P9-AGO-604

Decorated
Stoneware Pottery
of
North America

DISCARD

DONALD BLAKE WEBSTER

Decorated Stoneware Pottery of North America

CHARLES E. TUTTLE COMPANY
Rutland, Vermont

Representatives
Continental Europe: Boxerbooks, Inc., Zurich
British Isles: Prentice-Hall International Inc., London
Australasia: Paul Flesch & Co., Pty. Ltd., Melbourne
Canada: M. G. Hurtig Ltd., Edmonton

Published by the Charles E. Tuttle Company, Inc.
of Rutland, Vermont & Tokyo, Japan
with editorial offices at
Suido 1-chome, 2-6, Bunkyo-ku, Tokyo

Copyright in Japan, 1971, by Charles E. Tuttle Co., Inc.
Library of Congress Catalog Card No. 71-134032
International Standard Book No. 0-8048-0007-3

First printing, 1971

Printed in Japan

Contents

List of Illustrations

Acknowledgment is made to the following for permission to use photographs, as cited by number.

Albany Institute of History and Art, 121–23, 212, 241, 249, 259

Brink, Mr. and Mrs. Andrew, Hamilton, Ont., 159

British Museum, London, 4, 8–12

Brooklyn Museum, 16–17, 198, 206–7

Broome County Historical Society, Binghamton, N.Y., 70, 83, 293

Cone, Mrs. Tracy, Binghamton, N.Y., 226

Cortland County Historical Society, Cortland, N.Y., 54

Donald Everhart Winer Museum, Scranton, Pa., 35, 57, 74, 82, 84, 258

Henry Ford Museum, Dearborn, Mich., 147, 169, 177, 180, 197, 199, 244, 250, 257, 260, 270, 280–81

Henry Francis DuPont Winterthur Museum, Winterthur, Del., 52a–b, 66–67, 69, 86, 88–89, 90–93, 96, 101, 105, 116, 127, 148, 151, 167, 176a–c, 190–92, 194, 203, 213a–b, 224–25, 227–28, 230–32, 235, 246, 248a–b, 251–53, 255, 262–65, 268, 291

Luckert, Mr. and Mrs. Walter, Binghamton, N.Y., 38, 75, 110

McGill, Dr. and Mrs. William, Brantford, Ont., 132

Metropolitan Museum of Art, New York City, 39, 56, 87, 106, 200

Metropolitan Toronto and Region Conservation Authority, Toronto, 62, 65, 72, 85, 289

National Museum of Canada, Ottawa, 193

National Park Service, Washington, D.C., 5, 13, 14

New York Historical Society, New York City, 27, 182

New York State Historical Association, Cooperstown, N.Y., 63, 73, 76–77, 79–80, 98, 100, 104, 108–9, 111–13, 124, 126, 130, 133, 138–39, 144–45, 152–54, 156, 158, 160, 162, 175, 183, 186–89, 214 243, 295–300

North Carolina Development Commission, Raleigh, N.C., 19–20, 29

Ohio Historical Society, Columbus, 91, 95, 97

Old Sturbridge Village, Sturbridge, Mass., 135–36, 178, 210, 215a–b

Onondaga County Historical Society, Syracuse, N.Y., 50, 114, 294

Philadelphia Museum of Art, 24, 179a–c, 195–96, 221, 256

Remensnyder, Mr. John Paul, Saugerties, N.Y., 22, 30, 40–49, 51, 53a–b, 55, 59, 64, 102–3, 107, 115, 117–20, 125, 128–29, 131, 137, 149–50, 157, 161, 163–66, 168, 170–73, 185, 201–2, 204–5, 208–9, 211, 216–18, 220, 222–23, 233–34, 236–38, 240, 242, 245, 247, 254, 261, 269, 274–78, 282–88, 290, 292

Royal Ontario Museum, Toronto, 2, 3, 6, 7, 31, 142–43

Shelburne Museum, Shelburne, Vt., 61, 78, 99, 146

Smithsonian Institution, Board of Regents of the Smithsonian Institution, Annual Report, 1899, Department of the U.S. National Museum, Washington, D.C., 1901, 23, 25–26, 33

Snavely, Mr. William, McDonough, N.Y., 140–41

Victoria and Albert Museum, London, 1, 15

Weeks, Mr. and Mrs. Richard, Greene, N.Y., 81, 94, 155, 174, 181

Foreword

BY IVOR NOEL HUME

North American stoneware enjoys the curious distinction of being one of the most collected and yet neglected categories of ceramic antiques, and there has long been a need for a well-researched and profusely illustrated volume devoted to this important subject. In the absence of it, collectors have tended to acquire examples here and there without any real enthusiasm, simply because it was cheap and they realized that it should be represented in any collection of American ceramics. Vastly more pieces have been acquired by people who are not serious collectors, but who found them in junk shops and thought that they would look attractive on the patio. Thus, one finds butter jars serving as vases for molting bullrushes, or for the wet extremities of umbrellas. It is true that these gray stonewares were originally aimed at a comparably practical and popular market; but so, too, were most of the English white salt-glazed stonewares, Nottingham stonewares, delftwares, and slipwares, all of which now command the respect due to their rocketing monetary value as antiques. It is past time for North American stonewares to take their well-earned place in ceramic history, and it is to be hoped that Mr. Webster's book will contribute to that end.

The stoneware industry began in the Rhineland in the 15th century, and by the reign of Elizabeth I much of its output was being deliberately made for the export markets of France and England. So well received were the products that the importation into England of Rhenish stoneware shipped from the Netherlands and Flanders was deliberately excluded from the punitive Navigation Acts of the 17th and 18th centuries. They were still being imported into England, though in diminishing quantities, as late as 1776. The same types of blue and gray stoneware, generally comprising mugs, jugs, chamber pots, and smaller numbers of storage jars, were shipped out again from English ports to the American colonies up until the Revolution, and as Mr. Webster makes clear, it was this stoneware, and the immigrant potters who knew how to make it, that began the gray stoneware tradition that forms the substance of this book.

At no time did the American products aspire to the artistic heights scaled in the 16th and 17th centuries by the great Rhenish masters of Seigburg and Raeren, such as Knutgen, Emmens, and Mennicken, nor, for that matter, did they even equal the common Westerwald products of the first years of the 18th century. The creative glory of the Rhineland potters had faded long before the first of their offspring started work in America. Indeed, the products of the Cheesequake stoneware pottery in New Jersey in the 1770's are similar to the debased and purely utilitarian wares made in Flanders and the Rhineland in the same period. Ironically, the Gothic revival in Europe and England gave the Westerwald potters a new lease on life and brought forth a new class of stoneware cast in elaborate molds, aping the splendid creations of the late 16th and early 17th centuries. Thus,

Victorian Europe was deluged with a great variety of grotesque, cobalt-decorated gray stonewares whose purpose was purely decorative. However, this shift from the useful to the ornamental did not follow in America, where the potters stuck doggedly to their crocks and cuspidors—which was probably just as well.

The 19th-century European enthusiasm for Rhenish (largely Nassau) art stoneware also generated an interest in the earlier pieces from which it was copied. Out of that interest came M. L. Solon's classic two-volume work *The Ancient Art Stoneware of the Low Countries and Germany*. Published in 1892, it is much in need of revision based on subsequent discoveries, yet even now no one interested in the evolution of stoneware can afford to start any research without it. There is every reason to suppose that when Mr. Webster's book is that old, much the same will be said of it.

Preface

This book is concerned with that great mass and variety of North American pottery classified as salt-glazed stoneware. Found in every household on the continent in its own day, stoneware pottery served so many and such basic functions that it was simply taken for granted. Gradually replaced by other materials, and by the advances of environmental technology (particularly food preservation and packaging), salt-glazed stoneware finally passed from the scene, like so many obsolete domestic objects, unnoticed and unrecorded.

In our own time, however, collectors and antiquarians have increased vastly in number. The rapidly expanding economy since 1945 has given a relatively high standard of living to millions of people who could never have become collectors a generation or two earlier. With this increase in purchasing power there has also come both an intensification and broadening of antiquarian interests. Just as there are great numbers of collectors now who would not have been a half-century ago, so are there classes of 19th-

and even 20th-century objects which today are regarded as "antiques" in every sense, but would not have been considered "collectable" in earlier periods. There has perhaps even been a shift in popular collecting motivations—away from the narrow 19th-century connoisseurship, and more toward a concept of material or cultural history in a much more expansive sense.

As is explained in the following chapters, stoneware in North America was produced largely as utility and container pottery, and only rarely if ever as a fine ceramic or as a high decorative art. The salt-glazed container wares, however, as well as being made by a great number of producers all over the continent, were also a medium for simple and unsophisticated folk decoration in an endless variety of figures and motifs. It is these two characteristics, the range of makers' marks and the myriad decorations, which make salt-glazed stoneware as popular as it is today.

This book is essentially a survey both of the extent of North American stoneware forms and types, and geographical areas, and of the range and variety of decoration. The book is organized by subject categories of the decorations.

The great majority of stoneware, of course, bears rather simple and basic designs, and usually makers' marks as well. The focus of the illustrations, however, is necessarily toward the more elaborate and unusual decorations, which are by far the most interesting and sought after, but also the most uncommon.

I am indebted to a great many people and institutions who have aided me in this venture through a number of years. In the earliest stages the late Miss Dorothy Barck, librarian at the New York State Historical Association in Cooperstown, was of great help in locating research sources on New York State potters, and in making available manuscript material on the Clark potteries. Minor Wine Thomas, chief curator, provided photographs and permitted me to rephotograph slides of the Bassett collection in Cooperstown.

Mr. John P. Remensnyder of Saugerties, New York, allowed me to photograph all of the major pieces in his own large collection, and gave me benefit of his own knowledge of the stoneware potteries of the Hudson Valley, New York, and New Jersey. Later he read the draft manuscript, and provided in depth many valuable suggestions.

Ivor Noël Hume, director of archaeology at Colonial Williamsburg, both read the manuscript and offered the invaluable resource of his own broad knowledge and experience, and wrote the foreword.

Ian Quimby, registrar at the Henry Francis DuPont Winterthur Museum, provided photographs of a great many pieces in the Winterthur collection; Donald Shelley, director of the Henry Ford Museum, allowed me to photograph numbers of pieces in the collections there.

While working on this book, I have received a most cordial reception everywhere I have turned, and it is only unfortunate that I cannot mention here all of the individuals and museums who have offered pieces for illustration, and who have been generous of advice and support.

TORONTO   *Donald Blake Webster*

Decorated
Stoneware Pottery
of
North America

CHAPTER ONE

Origins and Basic Designs

The stream of ceramic history in Western Europe and North America has followed separate and often divergent paths. On the one hand, we have those potteries and later porcelains which assumed the status of fine arts. Many were in fact produced as artistic works and as examples of the ultimate potential of the potter's craft, with aesthetics foremost in mind. As a result, this pottery and porcelain has always received primary consideration, and early collector interest has played no small part in this attention.

Far more numerous, however, and recognized only recently, were potteries made not as works of art, essentially for exhibition or ego gratification, but for the mass of people and for daily use. This pottery—cottage, peasant, folk, naïve, country, call it what you will—was made in vastly varied forms, in large factories as well as in hundreds or thousands of small local potteries, with efficient fabrication, utility, and low cost as the primary considerations. Here decoration was secondary, and applied mainly to superimpose an aesthetic appeal on the utilitarian product. This was, then, pottery which reflected the needs and desires of the people who used it as much as the skills of the potters who produced it.

Thus we arrive at the folk tradition. In producing pottery types which became universally accepted, since they represented what large numbers of people needed as utensils for daily use, potters in every Western country tended toward very similar forms, often made with little or no change for generation after generation. As new materials and productive methods were developed and introduced, changes were of course unavoidable, but on the level of folk or utilitarian pottery the acceptance of and growth in popularity of new forms and materials was always gradual. So, too, there was inevitably a time lag between any innovation and its general acceptance, and this time gap tended to increase greatly with distance.

The country potters, however, like their clientele, were often very conservative, and deeply rooted in traditional methods and preferences. It was not usually the small potteries which initiated or readily accepted change; the individual potter more often than not had change forced upon him. But the potters who prospered, and even the many who just barely managed to survive, were men who could adapt, and recognized when they must. In the long run, however, it was not periodic change but a new technology, and pottery forms structured to industrial methods and equipment, that caused an almost total mortality. Again, very gradually, for the entire shift had many facets, the individual entrepreneurial potter, like so many individual craftsmen, could not possibly adapt and so simply disappeared.

Salt-glazed stoneware pottery from Europe was used in America from the earliest settlement, and began being made in a limited way in the early 18th century. Not until the late 18th century, however, did stoneware come into really universal manufacture in the United States—a period when it was already declining as a primary pottery type in Europe.

Stoneware then reached its zenith here as an applied art at about the time that it became a most unaesthetic and purely mechanically produced commodity in Europe. During the 19th century it became in North America the product of a vigorous craft with so many small and diversified producers that a full-fledged industry evolved. It flourished in a century when industrial technology was rapidly overtaking other crafts, and newer materials and methods had in Europe already overtaken the finer forms of salt-glazed stoneware. Even in America,

then, the last half-century of its existence was essentially borrowed time.

Thus American salt-glazed stoneware as a distinct pottery form was caught in the middle. As a decorative form, with rare exceptions, it never became, nor could it become, as fine or reach the state of excellence that it had in Germany during the 16th to 18th centuries, when stoneware was the hardest and most durable pottery known, or in England during the late 17th and 18th centuries. In fact, in an age when English creamware, porcelain, fine white stoneware, and later ironstone (all from essentially processed rather than wholly natural clays) dominated the American market for tablewares and finer potteries, 19th-century stoneware in North America could never get beyond a rather basic level.

Forced into its position as a largely utilitarian pottery, jugs, crocks, jars, and bottles—essentially storage vessels produced to sell at the lowest possible price—North American stoneware also became the medium for a form of decoration that had once, but in a very different way, been prevalent in Europe: pictorial incising and glazing. German common stoneware had invariably been decorated with glazed banding or area coloring, incised patterns, or relief designs. Prime and universal examples of the latter were the applied masks on German and English Bartmannkrüge, or bellarmine wine jugs.

The earliest American stoneware was essentially derived from the brown salt-glazed English and German Rhenish forms, often decorated with molded figures in relief. Stoneware of this type, often dipped or partially dipped in a thin brown slip before salt glazing, was made at the Andrew Duché Pottery in Philadelphia and the William Rogers Pottery at Yorktown, Virginia, after about 1725.

By the last quarter of the 18th century, however, the brown stonewares had largely been replaced by gray wares, which were salt glazed directly over the clay without underlying slip and often decorated with the later ubiquitous cobalt-oxide blue glaze traced or brushed on the surface. This type became dominant, and following the Revolution, with the establishment of numerous stoneware potteries in New England and New Jersey, blue-decorated gray stoneware came slowly into universal manufacture in the United States.

After roughly 1800, as new potteries filled ever growing markets as the population expanded and new areas became settled, a rather striking decorative form emerged—the incising in stoneware of often very intricate designs, flowers, animals and fish, and even full pictorial scenes. This period, from the end of the 18th century to about 1850, might be called the era of decorative incising, and it brought forth some of the handsomest pieces and most elaborate designs ever produced on American stoneware. This era of time-consuming incising, however, in the face of both competition and the ever increasing necessity for potters to produce efficiently and in quantity or go under, degenerated between 1840–60 to what we could well term the age of glaze painting.

Glaze painting became almost a fetish. Designs painted on the sides of unfired pottery in blue cobalt-oxide glaze had begun rather simply, in the fashion of the earlier incised designs. It did not take decorators long to discover, though, that it took little longer to paint an elaborate design than a simple one, and by 1860 the finest pieces coming out of potteries all over the Northeast were bearing designs that can only be called extravaganzas. Pictures in blue—flowers, forest scenes with animals, undirected but extreme decorative flourishes, and even human figures—occasionally covered whole sides of what were still primarily intended as plain storage jugs and crocks. The potters, rarely producing forms beyond basic utilitarian crockery, had obviously become carried away with themselves—but this is what today gives North American stoneware its flavor and appeal.

The shapes of American stoneware vessels in the earlier period were influenced very strongly by both earlier European forms and particularly by the great classical revival which, from about 1790 into the 1840's, greatly affected all material design, from architecture to furniture, from painting to pottery. Little American stoneware predating 1790 still exists today, most of it jugs and jars similar to the most simple of earlier German and English wares. After 1790, however, the classical revival dictated ancient Mediterranean shapes: strong ovoid forms and cyma curves became predominant. With small bases and heavy, somewhat top-heavy bodies, the pottery of the 1790–1820 period was forceful and striking even without additional decoration, with its clean lines and strong flowing curves. Filled and in use, however, it was also sometimes rather unstable.

As the 19th century progressed and the number of pottery makers became ever greater, the classic forms gave way, slowly and gradually, to more utilitarian and probably more easily produced shapes. Bases became wider and more stable; the curve of sides became flatter and less pronounced; and rims of jugs became heavier and less likely to chip.

By 1860, in virtually every area where stoneware was produced, stoneware shapes had come to one basic form, the cylinder. No longer were crocks or jugs even slightly bulbous, nor did potters attempt the finely curved surfaces of earlier days. Crocks now were completely straight sided, with substantial rims; jugs became cylinders with shoulders rounded into a heavily rimmed neck, and bottles, the earliest article to become universally uniform, became essentially a cone inverted on a cylinder.

This decline in salt-glazed stoneware as a product of the potter's craft, with the parallel trend toward uniform shapes and rapid semimechanized production, was accompanied by a last great spurt of quill-traced and painted blue-glazed decorating. Particularly in the Northeast, including Ohio, where competitive stoneware potteries were heavily concentrated, by 1865 or 1870 "pot painting" became almost a craze, with greater percentages of pottery than ever before now bearing at least some blue decoration. Though the occasional magnificent design emerged from this later period, the general decline affected decoration, too. In spite of quantity, the bulk of the designs were mechanical and superficial. Floral motifs, mere cursory passes with a glazing brush, are still of little note today; even the later bird decorations lack the boldness and character of earlier varieties.

Viewing stoneware with the fortunate benefit of hindsight, we become quickly aware of the effect of concentrations of potters, and essentially of business competition, on decoration. The earliest incised motifs, for example, appear on pieces from coastal New England, New York, and New Jersey, which was also the earliest area of salt-glazed stoneware manufacture sufficiently concentrated to arouse competitive instincts. From here the industry spread, following waterways, into interior New York, Pennsylvania, New England, and Ohio. Always with a time lag commensurate with distance, the earlier forms, shapes, and decorating techniques followed. Again, the majority of the earliest stoneware pieces produced in a given area were often quite plain; a substantial number of decorated pieces seemed to become common only when potters again approached market saturation.

In other areas, such as the Southeast, no great number of stoneware makers ever operated. Each potter here filled the needs of his own locale, large or small, without competition or any corresponding need to indulge in decorative work. Thus most Southeastern salt-glazed stoneware was absolutely plain; only occasional pieces were decorated, and then not heavily.

In eastern Canada there was again a long time lag in the beginnings of manufacture of stoneware, but little difference in the forms produced. For example, the first two stoneware potteries in Upper Canada, at Picton and Brantford, were established in 1849 by New York State potters William and Samuel Hart (at Picton) and Justus Morton, formerly of the Clark Pottery at Lyons, New York (at Brantford). Both potteries, and others established later, depended entirely on stoneware clay shipped from New Jersey. Thus Canadian salt-glazed stoneware, coming late, was also quite within the mainstream of the later Northeastern United States stoneware, although never as elaborately decorated.

Heavy salt-glazed stoneware in the first half of the 19th century filled a need that no other existing material could. Stoneware vessels, before canning and refrigeration, were ideal for storage, salting, and pickling. Inert to acids and alkalis, impervious to liquids, nothing else but wooden barrels could fill quite so many functions. Every household had crocks of salt beef or pork, pickled vegetables, or salted butter. Jugs and bottles kept vinegar, beer, whisky, and even water, cool, sweet, and drinkable—stoneware never tainted its contents.

By the late 1860's, however, came safe and reliable vacuum canning in glass jars; by the '70's came ice refrigerators and refrigerated transport of meats; and by the '80's, mass-molded, low-priced glass of all kinds. First in urban centers and then in the well-settled outlands, the individual housewife began to find less and less necessity to put up and store everything a family needed. This, of course, meant less call for stoneware storage vessels, and the immediate result—too many producers in a shrinking market—led first to frantic competition, and finally to the demise of smaller and weaker potteries. By the 1890's the character of stoneware pottery had changed completely, to an undecorated mechanically mass-produced commodity; by about 1910 the salt-glazed stoneware industry was dead.

Like most early commercial crafts or applied arts, salt-glazed stoneware making is gone forever. Like other crafts, however, it left behind it a good representation of its product—a pottery form which was once a mainstay and a staple of every rural household, store, tavern, and shop. A totally ubiquitous product, stoneware vessels were used with little change for a century and more. As a microcosm they reflect as directly on the whole stream of 19th-century life as they played an unconscious part of it.

As a folk or applied art form, the best salt-glazed stoneware, in form and decoration, may have been crude and often lacking in accepted artistic finesse, but it was expressive, forceful, and full of a life, flavor, and vigor all its own. That this inherent flavor and vigor in stoneware pottery can today transport us back to a long-gone rural frontier and recall school-day images of rugged life—the sturdy pioneer and his life of uncomplicated self-sufficiency—may well contain the nucleus of its appeal.

CHAPTER TWO

European Antecedents

Virtually all North American salt-glazed stoneware, though adapted to semi-industrial fabricating techniques and to 19th-century conditions, was derivative in that it was based on much earlier European forms and methods. European stoneware had, in fact, been imported into North America in considerable quantities since the early 17th century, and numbers of pieces continue to be found, particularly in excavations of early settlements and military sites. There was never a lack of use or appreciation of this most durable and impermeable form of common pottery, but its actual manufacture in the New World had to await the discovery of deposits of suitable clay, a gradual accumulation of knowledge of the complex and critical salt-glazing process, development of an adequate technological base, and a market beyond that which could be wholly served by imported wares.

Stoneware had existed in Europe, by way of Arab caravans trading from China, since the Middle Ages, and Chinese stoneware (or porcelains, after the Chinese definition of a ware that rings when struck) became a major trade commodity. There were, of course, continual efforts to copy the Chinese work, and probably by the 13th century German potters were producing basic utensils of stoneware. Rather than copying Chinese colored glazes, however, the Germans later developed a technique of salt glazing, whereby common salt, vaporized in the extreme heat of the firing kiln, combined chemically with silica in the body of the pottery to form an impervious and inert transparent glaze.

The Rhenish stonewares of the 17th and 18th centuries, which figured most heavily in trade to England and, by extension, the American colonies, largely took the form of containers and heavier utensils, particularly drinking mugs and tankards, chamber pots, and storage jars. Most common among the containers were handled wine bottles called Bartmannkrüge, brown salt-glazed pieces with bulbous, almost onion-shaped profiles, relatively long necks, and characteristic grotesque and bearded masks applied to, or impressed into, the bodies.

These stoneware Bartmannkrüge, of a material far superior to the rough earthenware jugs of late medieval and Renaissance Europe, became extremely popular and were exported in quantity. The smaller sizes were wine cruets or serving jugs, and hence table pieces; the larger versions, in identical shapes and forms, were general-purpose containers for storing liquids. The mottled brown salt glazing of the early molded wares, most notably from the Raeren area of the Rhineland, and the later Bartmannkrüge, was achieved by dipping the green pottery in a light brown slip prior to firing and salt glazing. The Raeren potters toward the late 16th century began to eliminate the brown slip (except on Bartmannkrüge), and instead commenced to produce gray salt-glazed wares decorated with cobalt-oxide blue.

Gray-bodied stoneware mugs and tankards, chamber pots, and jars, often with blue-glazed decorative work, became the other most common product of the Rhenish potteries. Applied decorations in relief were common, particularly foliage, masks, and seals. Incised work was often intricate and detailed, and done in combination with blue cobalt-oxide glazing—the origin of the incised and glazed decorating practiced in early 19th-century North America.

The primary stoneware-producing areas of Germany during the 16th century had been Raeren and Siegburg, on the lower Rhine. During the Thirty Years War (1619–48), however, the potters of this area migrated south to the Westerwald dis-trict to establish a new center for the stoneware industry; the Raeren potters settled largely in the Grenzhausen-Grenzau area, and those from Siegburg inhabited Höhr.

Generally from these areas, then, came the commoner salt-glazed stonewares made for export, primarily to England during the 17th and 18th centuries; many of the export forms were decorated specifically to appeal to an English market. By way of England, finally, came the Rhenish pottery, both brown and gray ware, which was so widely used in North America during the same period and which later so heavily influenced native American stoneware. Though never as light or as finely formed as the Chinese stonewares, the best of the early Rhenish work, heavily decorated and quite pleasing in a very Baroque manner, approached a real sophistication. It never, though, came close to achieving the stature of the 18th-century white stonewares and porcelains.

After more than a century of importation, the introduction of salt-glazed stoneware manufacturing into England appears first in a patent of 1671, obtained by John Dwight of Fulham. In this and a subsequent patent of 1684, Dwight claimed knowledge of the previously secret Rhenish salt-glazing process, and was granted exclusive rights to production in England. Typical of the fate of many early innovations, Dwight's patents and techniques were immediately and widely infringed, and during 1693–96 he commenced several suits in hopes of restraining his competitors. Foremost among them, or perhaps just the most adamant defendants, were John and David Elers, ex-silversmiths who had learned the stoneware craft at Cologne before coming to England in 1690.

Through the records of Dwight's suits, which have been fully explored several times, we find the names of some twenty stoneware makers, including late employees of Dwight. There is no doubt that stoneware of the German brown-glazed type (called Cologne-ware) was quite generally being made in England during the whole final quarter of the 17th century. While Dwight operated in Fulham, concentrating on fine earthenwares, he was also perhaps the first producer in England of brown-glazed stoneware—Bartmannkrüge, tankards, jugs, and other utensils. Competitors established potteries as well, producing an area type stoneware characterized by extremely freckled, dark brown over-slip or yellowish salt glaze.

During the same period Nottingham emerged as a stoneware center. Thomas Morley, named in the first Dwight suit, was working there in 1693, though the earliest known dated piece of Nottingham stoneware is marked 1700. The Nottingham work in general was lighter and more finely shaped than that of Fulham, and it was salt glazed in a lustrous and remarkably smooth brown, perhaps by the mixture of a lead-oxide glaze with the underlying brown slip.

Staffordshire, to which the Elers migrated in 1693, had long been a pottery producing area, and salt-glazed stoneware may well have been introduced there by Aaron, Richard, and Thomas Wedgwood, possibly in the late 1680's. The earliest manufactures were the typical gray and brown utensils, but the Elers had also brought alabaster molds for slip-casting, and metal stamps, which rapidly improved the range of products. Then, about 1720 when John Ashbury introduced white Devonshire clay and ground flint as an additive, Staffordshire moved rapidly away from the more basic and utilitarian gray and brown stonewares, and emerged as a center for production of fine and delicate white stonewares.

By 1700 salt-glazed stoneware was coming from other areas as well—Crich in Derbyshire, Chelsea, and Southampton (where, in fact, Symon Woolthus, senior and junior, may have made stoneware before Dwight's patent). The English ceramics industry, however, was in a stage of constant development and change, from the aspect of both materials and technology. First came Ashbury's white stoneware, a near porcelain, then Wedgwood's Queen's ware, and finally in the 19th century, ironstone "china." By the 1780's the greatest period of English salt-glazed stoneware as a fine pottery was over.

English utilitarian ware, the brown or partially brown slip-coated mugs, pots, jugs, and bottles, however, continued to be manufactured well into the 19th century. As earlier, these had been decorated with molded designs in relief, and often with incised or stamped inscriptions. In plainer form, some English brown stoneware, such as the ubiquitous India ink and shoe-blacking bottles, of which every North American antique shop has a goodly supply, were produced well into the present century.

Rhenish stoneware during the 19th and 20th centuries degenerated in quality, although not in design, to mass-manufactured mugs and tankards, press molded rather than hand turned, with crude baroque relief designs heavily colored with blue glaze or colored enamels. These pieces are, in fact, still being made, and salt glazing is still practiced in several areas in Germany. Today, however, in addition to the traditional tankards, a new dimension has been added —reproductions for North American consumption of early forms of American salt-glazed and blue-decorated crocks and jars.

As was mentioned in the first chapter, stoneware manufacture was late in coming to North America, certainly in part because of the ready availability of imported wares. So, too, the earlier American stoneware was logically patterned after familiar examples, that is, the Rhenish and English wares. It was not until the 19th century that purely American adaptations evolved.

One of the earliest known American stoneware potteries was that which William Rogers established at Yorktown, Virginia, probably in the late 1720's; it operated till 1739. From excavated examples, Rogers pottery was purely English in its form and technique, patterned directly after the Fulham type of brown-glazed work, and included the usual mugs and tankards, jugs, bowls, and pots, some quite finely formed and of high quality.

Another early stoneware pottery, producing in an apparently different tradition, was that of Andrew Duché, who operated in Philadelphia, also during the 1720's and '30's. Duché, however, produced gray salt-glazed wares with turned circumferal bands and decorated with blue cobalt-oxide glaze, in the Rhenish manner rather than the English. One shard excavated at Independence Square bears his marking, part of a tankard with an impressed stamp of the initials "A. D." at the base of the handle.

The ultimate direction of North American stoneware manufacture, which became quite evident as ever greater numbers of potters began operating toward the late 18th century, was toward adaptations of the Rhenish blue-decorated and gray-bodied wares, rather than the brown-glazed Fulham forms. Occasionally brown-glazed wares in the English tradition were produced, to be sure, but they were always exceptional, and never became a primary product of the North American container and utility stoneware industry.

In the earlier period, the late 18th and very early 19th centuries, American stoneware was very like the simplest and most basic of the Rhenish types—similar vessel shapes, similar incised and blue-filled rudimentary decoration, and similar productive techniques. Evolution to somewhat more indigenous American forms, and more particularly to indigenous decorative styles, proceeded partially, perhaps, because of the quite different American culture and environment, and most certainly very largely due to the influence of a growing machine technology. Thus in time there developed a rather unique North American ceramic type based on, but in many ways totally unlike, any of its European predecessors.

1. An extreme example of floral relief decorating, this Rhenish Bartmannkrug or bellarmine from the Cologne area dates from the mid-16th century. As well as the characteristic applied mask, and other small vignettes, the intricacy of the individually applied leaves and stems is particularly notable. A piece such as this represents the highest form of the earlier German utilitarian stoneware. Victoria and Albert Museum, Crown Copyright.

2. The earlier Bartmannkrüge were more bulbous and even in typical examples were often more ornate than later versions. Probably a Cologne piece, this eight-inch-high bottle of the late 16th or early 17th century is decorated with three applied escutcheons as well as the bearded mask. Royal Ontario Museum.

3, 4. These two Bartmannkrüge are typical of those 17th and 18th century wine jugs made in great quantity in both Germany and England. That in Plate 3 (left) dates from the late 17th century, and was found in London. Seven inches high, with the characteristic mask and round medallion on the body, it could be either German or English. Royal Ontario Museum. The piece in Plate 4, eight and one-eighth inches high, was found in 1864 when a long-closed vault was opened at Dwight's Fulham Pottery. British Museum, Crown Copyright.

5. Andrew Duché of Philadelphia was perhaps the earliest American maker of gray-bodied, blue-decorated stoneware in the Rhenish manner. This base-fragment of a tankard, excavated at Independence Square, has a blue-glazed circumferal band around the base, and is impressed with the initials "A.D." in a cartouche. National Park Service.

6. Rhenish gray salt-glazed tankards, this one missing its probable original pewter cover, commonly combined incised and pressed or applied decorations (here diamonds in relief) with the use of blue cobalt-oxide glazes. A typical Westerwald area piece, the tankard dates c. 1700. Royal Ontario Museum.

7. This Westerwald tankard of the mid-18th century includes both incised and impressed decorations, and blue glazing, but is without applied reliefs. With its pewter cover, it is illustrative of a form which, now molded, is still being made. The decorative methods and styles are the direct ancestor of those which were universally applied to North American stoneware during the first half of the 19th century. Royal Ontario Museum.

8. Plain tavern tankards were as basic a product of the English potteries as of the Rhenish. This gray-bodied piece, without blue decoration, has only a plain wheel-turned banding. The crowned "A. R." (Anne Regina 1702–14) was a capacity marking. British Museum, Crown Copyright.

9, 10. Common mugs, typically globular with wide cylindrical necks, were produced by most of the early English salt-glaze potteries. The mug in Plate 9 (left) has the freckled brown glaze, as here sometimes with drip marks, characteristic of the Fulham potteries. The marking, for standard capacity, is a crowned "W. R." (William III, 1688–1702). British Museum, Crown Copyright. The higher necked piece in Plate 10 has the smooth and lustrous brown glaze of the Nottingham stonewares. The applied ornaments are three crowns surrounding a medallion, with a bust of Queen Anne (1702–14) and the initials "A. R." British Museum, Crown Copyright.

11, 12. English tankards with molded relief decorations, and usually dipped or half dipped in brown slip before salt glazing, were an extremely popular form during the 18th century, and well into the 19th. The piece in Plate 11 (right) bears in relief hunt scene, rosettes, trees, and arms of the Blacksmiths' Company, with the incised inscription "P. M. / 1720." British Museum, Crown Copyright. The later piece, in Plate 12, impressed "Phillips / 1775," also bears a hunt scene, and a molded and applied panel after William Hogarth's series of engravings entitled "Modern Midnight Conversations." British Museum, Crown Copyright.

13. William Rogers, the "poor potter" of Yorktown, began making stoneware in the English style probably before 1730. Among Rogers' finest pieces were his small bowls, also basically English, which were thin walled and finely formed. Like the mugs, this piece was partially dipped in brown slip before firing and salt glazing, and was found in Williamsburg, Virginia. National Park Service.

14. Examples of Rogers' work given here are, at top, a sagger (firing container) for one quart mugs, and sections of two mugs with applied swans in relief. Both mugs were made for the Swan Tavern in Yorktown, and found at the site. In the foreground is the top of a jug of the bellarmine type. National Park Service.

15. Salt-glazed stoneware as an art was in decline by the mid-18th century. This English jug, perhaps from Fulham, in its medallions and inscriptions shows good 18th-century humor, but in its shape and construction begins to approach the mass-produced and completely plain container stoneware of the 19th century. It is clearly a transitional piece. The jug as inscribed contained "Iron Peartree Water . . ." from a spa for the gout-ridden ". . . near Godstone, Surrey." The left-hand applied medallion shows a man with crutches under the heading "Oh, the Gout"; on the visible right medallion he throws away his crutches under the noble inscription "Drink and be Well." Victoria and Albert Museum, Crown Copyright.

16, 17. Excavated shards are the best indicator of the overall production of early potteries, and also serve to identify existing pieces. The group of shards in Plate 16 (left) is from the James Morgan Pottery at Cheesequake, New Jersey, c. 1775–85. All indicate pottery done in the Rhenish manner—salt glaze over a gray body and decoration in blue cobalt-oxide. One shard is dated 1776. The group in Plate 17 (below) is from the Warne & Letts Pottery at Cheesequake, c. 1800–1813, and the shards show general use of coggled and stamped decoration. Brooklyn Museum.

CHAPTER THREE

The Arts of the Potter

All forms of pottery are classified basically not by their glazes, forms, or finishes, but by their hardness and the characteristics and composition of the clays of which they are formed. The essential dividing line separates soft from hard bodied pottery in relation to the hardness of iron—whether plain iron will scratch the fired pottery, or whether a piece of the pottery will scratch iron. In essence, too, the hardness of a finished piece of pottery depends largely on the presence and relative amounts of two essential components: silica and kaolin (decomposed feldspar), often referred to as alumina in early technical works.

Stoneware is essentially a vitreous or vitrified pottery, meaning simply that it has a dense body which even in unglazed form will not absorb water. Stoneware is also extremely hard; it will strike sparks from steel, and will ring very much like glass when struck.

Successful stoneware making, of course, depended primarily on the initial clay, but good stoneware clay was unfortunately not available locally in most areas of the country. Clay for brick or plain red earthenware was almost universal, but virtually every stoneware pottery in New England and New York imported its clay, the highest quality generally from Amboy, New Jersey, and a somewhat lower quality and lower-priced clay from Long Island. Since raw, damp clay is certainly a bulky and heavy commodity to transport, it seems strange at first that so many stoneware potteries were established in the first half of the 19th century in areas remote from the supply of essential raw material, but in fact the problem of transportation was not what it might have seemed.

The largest and most productive potteries in terms of quantity were generally located at least in proximity to navigable water. The potteries of Bennington, Albany, Fort Edward, and Troy, for example, were clustered near the Hudson River, which made relatively simple the shipment not only of raw clay from New Jersey but also the wide distribution of finished pottery. Nathan

Clark, who started his great pottery in 1805 at Athens, New York, on the Hudson below Albany, bought clay by the sloopload, from Morgan's Bank at Amboy, New Jersey and Long Island, both which delivered to his docks. Shiploads of clay would go as well to any and all the coastal or navigable river cities of New England, the Middle Atlantic states, and Canada.

New canal systems, particularly the Erie and its tributaries, after 1820 made stoneware potteries possible virtually everywhere, for clay could be loaded in large canal boats at South Amboy and shipped throughout New York State and even the Great Lakes regions.

Nathan Clark continually shipped supplies to his subsidiary potteries at Lyons and Mount Morris, New York; one recorded order for shipment to Lyons by canal indicates as well the prime materials used by stoneware potteries. The "load" unit was probably a wagonload.

300 loads Morgan's best [clay]
 75 loads Long Island [clay]
  1 load [Albany] slip clay
 75 Bu. White Sand
 25 lbs. P. Blue (FFFg if possible) [Fine granulated cobalt-oxide called "powder blue"]

Overland transport by wagon, possible for short distances, was very expensive and thus limited. Thomas Chollar of Cortland, New York, for example, brought New Jersey clay to Syracuse via the Hudson River and Erie Canal, and then by wagon for the final thirty miles south to Cortland.

The single factor of available water transportation defined the areas in which stoneware potteries could successfully operate. The necessity for any overland transport of clay, of course, both raised the cost and restricted the amount. Potteries such as Chollar's were thus among the smaller operations, and often the first to disappear in the face of competition.

Some potters, of course, to cut costs and increase production, adulterated purchased clay with the local product, most generally a rough red brick clay. This was often done to the very limit possible, consistent with retaining a clay capable of enduring the firing temperatures necessary for making true stoneware. The quality of the end product reflected the clay mixture; low quality stoneware was both porous and fragile.

. The clay from Amboy or Long Island, after perhaps a month in transit, arrived at the pottery raw and unpurified, and nearly completely dry. Before it could be used this clay had to be restored to a plastic state by mixing with water, then purified by screening out pebbles and hard lumps, and finally mixed with whatever additives were called for, including white quartz sand to provide additional bulk, and a binder that prevented later cracking and breaking.

A machine called a pug-mill was used to break up and mix the dry clay with water and sand. In its simplest form, the pug-mill was a cylindrical wooden tank with iron spikes projecting from the inner walls. A vertical central shaft, also with projecting and interleaving spikes, could be turned by horse or water power, acting much like a very slow beater or mixer. The dry or perhaps already plastic clay was dumped into the pug-mill, and water and sand were added in the correct proportions as the spiked shaft was turned, until the clay, by then viscous, was completely homogenized. The cylinder could then be emptied from the bottom, and the semifluid clay worked through screens to remove stones and solid lumps.

The clay, made ready for the potter's wheel, was in a plastic and pliable but not fluid state, and the job of forming jars, crocks, jugs, bottles, and a variety of other utensils from it went to the "thrower." A master potter, and the most important of the specialized craftsmen in any pottery, the "thrower" took a glob of clay (he knew from long experience just about how much) and literally threw it on his flat and horizontal potter's wheel so that it would stick. Turning the wheel base with his feet, counterclockwise so that the clay as he shaped it wedged against his right hand, he then quickly centered the lump of clay and began to shape a crock or jug.

First hollowing out the lump as the wheel revolved at a considerable speed, the thrower, with wet hands and using wooden ribs and scrapers, began to shape and raise first the walls of the piece from the bottom, and then to form a rim or begin to constrict the top into the neck of a jug. The whole process of rough-shaping the crock or jar took probably no more than two or three minutes, and the thrower had to be a fast worker as well as a skilled one, for he often had to turn several hundred pieces a day.

A thrower, in a pottery which was essentially a small factory to produce identical forms in quantity, needed a precise eye, for his measuring tools were few. A simple height gauge, perhaps a stick mounted to project over his wheel, would regulate the vertical dimensions of his work; calipers or a fixed gauge could guide diameter. Beyond these basic exterior measuring devices, the thrower's eye for form and shape, and his fingers and sense of tactile judgment of the thickness of bottoms and sides of vessels, were all important.

In the larger potteries the various operations were more specialized than in small establishments where the proprietor, with a couple of helpers, did everything from throwing to decorating and firing. The thrower, as a specialist, formed his pieces just slightly thicker and heavier in rough dimensions than they would be as finished pieces, using his variety of properly cut wood or ceramic ribs and smoothers to shape curves and rims. He would then move to another wheel, on which an apprentice or helper had perhaps already placed another glob of clay.

In the thrower's place a turner or finisher would take over, first carefully smoothing the jar or crock inside and out with a wet cloth (the final transparent salt glaze would not hide imperfections in the clay). The finisher would then apply whatever banded coggled decoration was called for, pressing his handled coggle wheel, perhaps from a rest for steadiness, against the slowly turning wet pot till the design had been impressed fully around, hopefully joining the beginning.

Handles were applied to nearly all stoneware pieces. In earlier periods they might be formed by simply rolling a rope of clay between the palms. In the 19th century all but elaborate molded handles were usually extruded by forcing clay from an opening at one end of a press or tube—much like a baker's pastry tube. The clay rope, round, triangular, or ovoid, was then simply cut to proper lengths and pressed onto the finished piece with the finisher's thumbs. At the largest potteries, there might even be a specialist "handler" who did nothing but extrude, cut, and apply handles. A final smoothing with a wet cloth and the pot was ready for drying, with perhaps five minutes having elapsed since it had begun as a lump of clay. The final operation was to impress the wet clay with a hand stamp bearing the name of the pottery or proprietor, or the stamp of a major purchaser.

In smaller potteries, finished pieces were lined up on boards, eight or ten or twelve pieces to a board, and carried out to dry in the sun. At night, of course, they had to be carried back to a shed, and in bad weather drying took a long time. Thus larger operations, and (weather being unreliable) most potteries as time went on, dried their pottery in drying ovens, wood-fired low-temperature ovens close to the pottery-forming area. Depending on the temperature, it took one to three days for the plastic clay to dry into what is known as greenware, dry but unfired clay that was fragile, brittle, and easily crumbled.

The first treatment of greenware, before decorating or firing, was a washing inside with what is called Albany slip. Differing from glazes, which were essentially metallic oxides and silica, slips were fine clays, mixed in solution until liquid. Albany slip in particular was a brown or black clay first mined (and still mined) from the Hudson River near Albany, New York; it was used in solution as a wash, and after firing as a lining on the insides of virtually all North American stoneware after 1800 or 1805. The rationale was simply that, as pottery was stacked for firing base to base and rim to rim, salt glazing would not affect the sealed insides. A separate and stable inside surface coating was needed, and the brown Albany clay was not only an excellent lining but it was also readily available.

Once the clay was judged dry, it was ready for the decorators with glazes and enamels, or if it was to be incised, the pottery had been decorated before completely drying. Since decorators will be discussed at length in the following section, let us assume that the greenware, already decorated, is ready for firing, the most critical operation of all.

Stoneware, unlike red earthenware, required a maximum temperature of about 2300 degrees Fahrenheit, actual white heat, to fuse the formed clay-sand mixture into a hard, dense pottery. The whole operation, by necessity done in a large, brick-lined, thick-walled, and earth-covered kiln which was fueled with wood, took about six to eight days. Since the kiln had to be watched, checked, and periodically fueled day and night, it was rather expensive from the labor standpoint, and the kiln was loaded in such a way as to fire every piece that could possibly be fitted in.

The insides of the pottery had already been washed with Albany slip; only the outsides of the vessels were to be salt glazed. The greenware was stacked in tiers or courses, placed precisely mouth to mouth and base to base, sometimes six or eight pieces high, a relatively heavy column. Had the usual shape not been basically conical or cylindrical, with inherent structural strength, the pieces on the lowest level would probably never have withstood the weight, but in fact they usually did.

The kiln held anything from several hundred to a thousand pieces at a firing—a week's production of a thrower and a finisher. There was always some time lag, for the greenware was always thoroughly air dried before it was stacked in the kiln, and the potter thus had to maintain a backlog ready for firing. The kiln was not fired until it was full, and great numbers of existing pieces of stoneware, dented, malformed, or with sides slightly buckled by weight, indicate the weight that was piled up and the almost white heat that sometimes returned the pottery to a near plasticity. At too high a temperature, pieces could easily, and often did, become dented or buckled, as the components of the clay first fused as intended, but then began to melt. These pieces were discarded or sold in the end as seconds at reduced prices.

The pottery stacked in the kiln rested on setting tiles, roughly rectangular, triangular, or sometimes doughnut-shaped pieces of stoneware that were made quickly to be used as separators, but could be used over and over again. Then to make the vertical stacks more stable, the kiln loaders inserted pieces of raw clay, simply squeezed out by hand, between the pots so that the clay lumps touched each piece of pottery at only a single small contact point, which of course would not be touched by the later salt glazing. These lumps of clay, fired and salt glazed with the pottery, were variously termed cockspurs, wedges, or saggers, and since they could not be used again, were usually thrown aside. Today both setting tiles and cockspurs are found in great numbers whenever an early stoneware site is excavated.

The kiln was closed up and a fire started underneath. First the temperature was brought up only to about the boiling point of water, and kept there for a time. This allowed all remaining moisture in the greenware to evaporate off; if the temperature built up too rapidly, this moisture would form steam and crack the pottery.

Slowly and steadily, with the fire spread over the entire firebox and fresh wood always spread evenly, the temperature in the kiln was raised to about 2200 or 2300 degrees Fahrenheit—it was not precisely measurable. An experienced kilnman, rather, judged the temperature by eye—looking at the color of the burning pottery through a viewing hole. The raising of the temperature to the maximum took as long as two days, for the fire could only be built up very slowly. Throwing on too much wood at one time might increase the flames once it started burning, but initially it would partially smother the fire and cause a temporary drop in the kiln temperature. A rapid temperature drop, however short, at best would likely cause discolorations in the finished pottery; at worst it could cause a great deal of the pottery to crack.

Once the kiln had been brought to full temperature, the pottery was ready for salt glazing, the process that had originated in Germany in the 12th or 13th century. Like so many other pottery-making operations, by the 19th century salt glazing was such common knowledge among potters, though each was often secretive, that the exact procedure was rarely written down. The fire was fueled again until it burned with a full blaze. Then the top of the kiln was opened and the glazers shoveled common rock salt directly down into the heat. No exact amount was required, too little would suffice and too much would do no harm, but a bushel or so would do the job. The kiln opening was then quickly closed up again.

Most potters tended to be rather close mouthed about their glaze mix recipes and glazing processes, but about 1835 Nathan Clark wrote out a list of rules of stoneware procedure practiced at his potteries, probably for the guidance of new employees.

Rules for Making & Burning Stoneware

1st. Let the wheel man be careful to have every piece run exactly true on the wheel. Make them of a kind precisely of the same height & width. Have the same turned [by the] light hands [of a man] finisher. Shape smooth inside & outside, the bottom a suitable thickness and a good top.

2nd. Let it be handsomely handled & smoothly polished in proper season [sequence].

3rd. Let the ware when dry be carefully set in . . . [illegible in ms] . . . in this last washed and blued [lined inside with Albany slip; decorated outside].

4th. Let the plate be well made. Kiln cleaned out and mended in complete order for setting.

5th. Care must be taken to set the courses [of pottery] straight—one piece exactly over another.

6th. Have your wood in good order. Raise your fire progressively, neither too fast nor too slow. Examine well and understand the management of your kiln so as to heat all parts alike. Be careful not to throw your wood in the [fire] too soon or do any other act that may have a tendency to retard the heat. When fit to glaze have your salt dry. Scatter it well in every part of your kiln. During this act you must keep a full and clear blaze so as to accelerate the glazing and give the ware a bright gloss. Stop it perfectly tight and in six days you may draw a good kiln of ware.

The salt, on hitting the 2300-degree heat, vaporized almost instantaneously, and the sodium vapor in effect combined with and covered every exposed surface in the kiln—the sides of every piece of stoneware and the walls of the kiln itself. The resulting glaze, however, was not simply a layer of condensed salt over the pottery. Actually the salt, sodium chloride, in vaporizing gave off its chlorine, which either dissipated as a free (and poisonous) gas, or occasionally recondensed as hydrochloric acid. The vaporized sodium, however, combined with the usually rather high silica content of the stoneware clay (and perhaps the aluminas too) to form a hard surface layer of a form of sodium silicate, a virtually impermeable and insoluble glaze. Not all of the salt vaporized, of course; much simply fell to the floor of the kiln.

Once the salt-glazing process was completed, the fires were kept burning at a high temperature for about three or four more days to complete the fusion of the body of the pottery, and then slowly reduced. The kiln had to be cooled as slowly and evenly as it had been initially heated up, so that the whole firing process took from six to eight days. Only then could the kiln be opened and the finished stoneware removed.

Depending on the attentiveness and judgment of whoever supervised the firing, the kiln load of pottery could be either a complete success or a total loss. Obviously a great many mishaps could occur, and there was always a certain amount of wastage or breakage, which over years resulted in great pottery dumps of broken shards, badly buckled pottery, setting tiles and cockspurs, old kiln-lining tiles or firebrick, and masses of miscellaneous matter. Hopefully, though, most of the pottery did survive all of the operations and hazards inherent in its manufacture, and was carried and sold throughout the potter's area.

18. The usual pug-mill at a small pottery, for pulverizing and mixing clay, was a vertical cylinder with rotating central shaft. Both the cylinder and shaft had projecting spikes, so that the machine was, in effect, a huge mixer. This drawing of an industrial pug-mill, dating about 1875, shows the basic internal arrangement. This mill has spikes projecting only from the central shaft. The gear arrangement was coupled to the power source, a water wheel or steam engine.

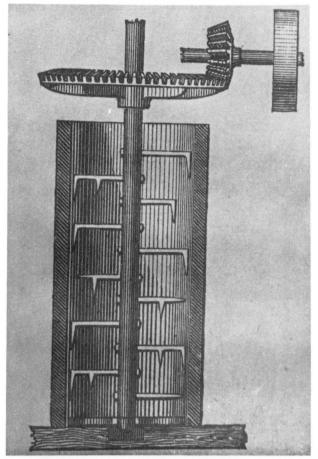

19. This pug-mill, in use at the Jugtown Pottery in North Carolina, is powered by a mule pulling a horizontal beam to turn the shaft. North Carolina Development Commission.

20. Throwing identical pieces on the potter's wheel required experience, and a good eye and strong hands for shaping the clay. Though most potters' wheels are now rotated by electric motors, other techniques have changed little or not at all over the centuries. The thrower is Ben Owen, at the Jugtown Pottery in North Carolina. North Carolina Development Commission.

21. Two types of wheels appear in this 15th-century woodcut, one hand powered and long since obsolete; the other, rotated by the thrower's foot, was ancient even then and is still the most common manually powered wheel.

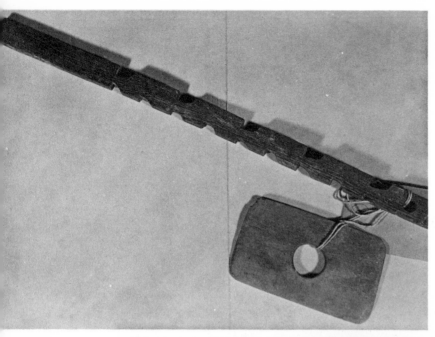

22. Throwers used a great variety of simple wooden shaping tools. The rectangular piece with finger hole is a rib, probably for smoothing the angle between the inside bottom and walls of crocks or jugs. The longer notched stick is a scraper for forming and shaping the rims of crocks or lips of bottles. Collection of Mr. John Paul Remensnyder.

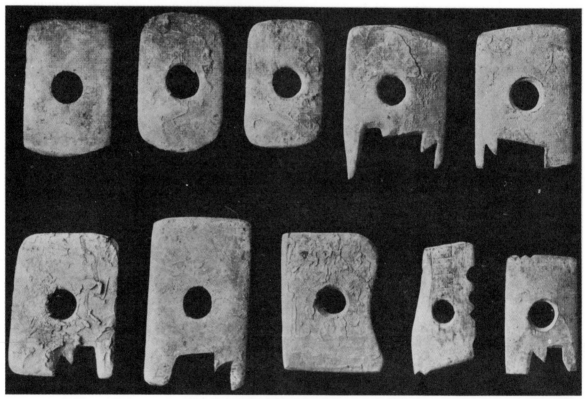

23. These ribs, made of wood but clay covered, were used for a variety of shaping operations, including curves and corners. Note particularly the five ribs notched for forming different rim types, probably unique to this pottery. With numerous other potter's tools, these pieces are from the Thompson Pottery, *c.* 1785–1890, at Morgantown, West Virginia. Smithsonian Institution.

24. For making the decorative banding which appears on many early stoneware pieces, the finisher used a small tool called a coggle. The design was cut or cast in a small wood or clay rotating wheel, this one wooden, attached to a handle with a pin. To coggle a band, the finisher held the wheel against a wet pot as it rotated slowly on the potter's wheel, pressing the design into the clay. Philadelphia Museum of Art.

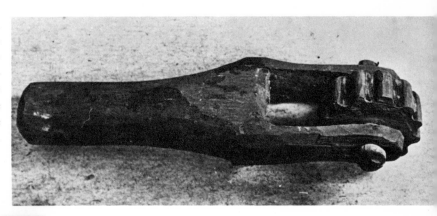

25. Particular designs for decorative banding were often unique to specific potteries, and if a banding design can once be established to a pottery, it can be very useful for attributing other existing but unmarked pieces. These coggles and the extra rollers are of molded and baked clay and were mounted in the handles on wooden pins. The two flat-surfaced pieces are clay hand-stamps for impressing single motifs. All are from the Thompson Pottery. Smithsonian Institution.

47

26. Handle-forming dies were fitted to a press, which forced out a long rope of clay with a shaped cross section. Pieces were then cut to proper length for attaching as handles. These dies, from the Thompson Pottery, are made of varied materials—the top two, left center, and center pieces are pottery, the right center die is sheet iron, and the lower two are oak blocks faced with tacked-on sheet iron. Smithsonian Institution.

27. The final step, stamping the finished pot with the firm name, was done with a hand stamp that impressed wooden, lead printers' type, or fired clay letters into the body of the pot. This stamp, a cast lead printing block, pressed "C. Crolius / Manufacturer / New-York" on the work of Clarkson Crolius, Jr., from c. 1838–1850. New York Historical Society.

28. The typical stoneware (and red earthenware) kiln was built below ground, so that only the top of the earth-covered dome could be seen from above. Fires were fueled from a pit or on occasion even from a tunnel. The holes near the top of the kiln were kept plugged except during the process of salt glazing.

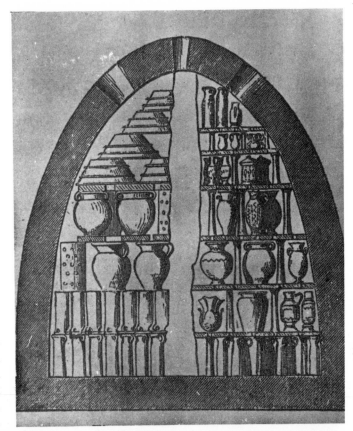

29. The Jugtown Pottery's production is fired in a brick kiln, here being loaded with greenware. Note how the handles have been applied. The man inside the kiln will stack the courses of jars base to base and top to top. North Carolina Development Commission.

30. Setting tiles and cockspurs were pieces of rough stoneware, rectangular, triangular, or just unshaped pieces of clay, used as separators and props between pieces of greenware in the kiln. Some pieces were used only once; others could be used many times. The sites of most early potteries, even today, are littered with these separators. These are from the Morgan Pottery in New Jersey. Collection of Mr. John Paul Remensnyder.

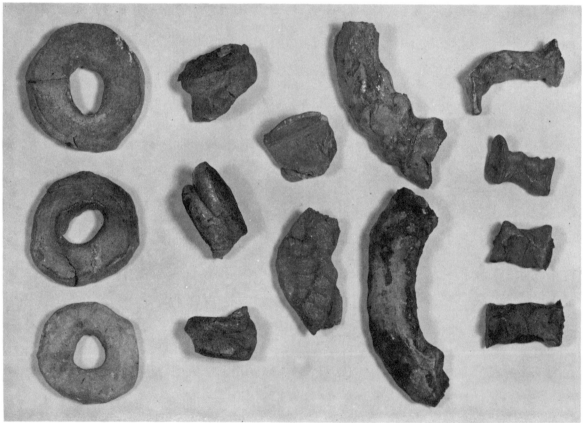

31. From a much later operation than the Morgan Pottery, these setting tiles, both flat and doughnut shaped, and wedges, cockspurs or saggers, were recently excavated (and appeared in great quantity) at the site of the stoneware pottery at Brantford, Ontario, 1849–c. 1905. These pieces date from the 1860's or '70's. Royal Ontario Museum.

CHAPTER FOUR

The Arts of the Decorator

The actual craft of conceiving, forming, and producing stoneware pottery was the province of throwers, finishers, and kiln workers. Particularly in earlier periods, however, when the classically pure and smooth shapes and lines of this pottery were solely creations of the potters' own imagination and skills rather than, as after 1850 or 1855, primarily products of a new industrial technology, stoneware was often an artistic form in itself. To have permanent value, however, any product of an art or craft must stimulate lasting interest and desirability, and represent the best of its period and type. Desirability, to the contemporary antiquarian, is most often a result of both rarity and the fact that early stoneware, much like country furniture and early ironwork, projects the all-pervasive flavor of our own domestic past—an aura of farm and fireside, of a simpler life in a romantic age. North American pottery of all types, not only stoneware but all earthenwares as well, provides its own inherent imagery, and needs no artificial interpretation.

Early but absolutely plain pieces of stoneware, more than likely by unknown makers, will still have a great appeal through their varied shapes, part and parcel of the North American classical revival, perhaps most overtly expressed in the early 19th century by the renaissance of classical Greek and Roman architecture. Far more than from its varied but extremely subtle shapes or specific rarity, however, the best of North American stoneware has achieved lasting desirability and won particularly a broad appreciation through its decorations. These are a myriad of incised and glazed designs which, unlike the monochromatic pottery itself, instantly intrude on the awareness and can gain at least the interest of virtually everyone. From an initial awareness and appreciation of these designs can come an understanding in depth of the pottery itself.

The decorating of stoneware, with designs incised or pressed in the wet clay and/or glazed in blue on the dried greenware, goes back to the earliest production of this form of pottery in North America. The basic influences which early determined both the fact and often the form of stoneware decoration were European. American stoneware decorators, however, soon became influenced more by their own domestic environment than by an increasingly distantly removed tradition, taking as the primary source of their creations the plants and animals around them as well as man-made objects and basic political, social, and cultural influences on their personal lives. Designs varied from elaborate sailing ships, patriotic eagles, or wild animals to human figures, birds and natural scenes, or simple floral motifs that in their least complex form were nothing more than a few brushstrokes of blue glaze. The great majority of stoneware designs can readily be categorized into a few groupings, since at least similar motivations were expressed, though in vastly different ways, by decorators everywhere. At the same time, it would be equally safe to say that anything which could possibly be applied pictorially to stoneware appeared at one time or another.

In smaller potteries, and most particularly during the 18th and early 19th centuries, the potters themselves were usually also the decorators, completing each piece from a lump of clay to the final incised decoration and coggled band, in a unified operation. The one-man operation or handcraft organization, however, was hardly conducive to quantity production and not very economically stable. In this increasingly complex industry, specialization of operations was essential, first for growth and finally for plain day-to-day survival. Thus by mid-century larger and more financially viable potteries had adopted by necessity the more modern form of organization in which proprietors were business managers, throwers and finishers specialized in primary production, and decorators provided an entirely separate subsidiary skill.

Stoneware pottery, as a primarily utilitarian form, was mentioned only occasionally in contemporary 19th-century sources, and then it was often deprecatingly; virtually no documentation exists on the craft of the stoneware decorator. Most technical knowledge concerning working with plastic or dried clay as a medium and the usage of incising stylus, slip-cup, and glazing brush was imparted from master to pupil, and the latter grew increasingly skilled in time. The little available evidence suggests, however, that the system of formal and legal indenture or apprenticeship did not apply to stoneware decorating as it did to most manual crafts. More likely an informal on-the-job training situation was responsible for not only what little training a decorator did receive but for the continuance of standard designs at different potteries for much longer periods than single individuals could be expected to remain productive.

Apprentices in most crafts were teen-age boys, but few boys possessed the manual dexterity to execute smoothly and quickly designs that often required considerable imagination in concept, as well as an inherent manual ability, beyond whatever skill minimal training could provide. Neither did boys have the essential patience.

Not only were most decorators adults, but at least after the stoneware industry had progressed to a point of elimination of the smallest and least stable potteries, there is reason to believe that a good percentage of productive decorators were artistically inclined women—working perhaps on a part-time and piecework basis. Generalization would be very premature, but the writer has traced, from verbal recollections of people who knew them or of them, individual decorators at five different New York State stoneware potteries during the late 19th century—all were women.

As a purely superficial but strong impression, it would appear that during the period of incising as the primary decorating technique the great majority of decorators were men, many of them potters and proprietors as well. Once surface-glazed designs, beyond the simplest formless decorations, became dominant (let us say from 1840 to 1845) the balance began to shift, until by the latter half of the 19th century many decorators were women. Perhaps women, well known to have a greater manual dexterity than men, were better able to rapidly execute often complex surface-glazed designs. So, too, women are often more adept than men at extremely intricate work, and unlike the vast majority of early incised designs, as the century progressed surface-glazed decorations became increasingly detailed and elaborate.

The decorators who applied designs to stoneware, whatever their sex, were not artists in the accepted sense of painters or sculptors who usually have rigorous train- ing with a foremost emphasis on self-expression. Rather the decorators, consciously and explicitly at least, were simply applying increased sales appeal to purely utilitarian products. In their better and more deliberate work, however, many decorators created that form of implicit, culturally and environmentally oriented expression which today we call folk art. With little education, untraveled, largely untrained, and usually products of narrow and limited environments, rural or urban, stoneware decorators were certainly true "folk" by any definition. Their work often shows great imagination beyond prerequisite technical skills, yet the expressiveness and imagery does not at all depend on manual skill; many of the most pleasing and perceptive designs are crude in their execution. Some designs indicate real environmental insight, far oftener a fine sense of humor, as well as occasional manifestations of apparent alcoholism or mental aberrations. The mainstream of stoneware decoration, however, is above all a reflection of the power of 19th-century romanticism, even in areas and among people far removed from the mainstream of American thought—a strong optimistic nationalism, particularly in the designs of eagles, patriotic symbols, and warships, and a strong sympathetic feeling toward the rural life and the wonders and beauties of nature, not nature as a plum for development, but nature as a vast untrammeled and endless entity before which the works of man were insignificant. This was an age of biblical literalism, of Jeffersonian agrarianism and Jacksonian popular democracy, of military conquest and westward expansion; and superimposed on all was a belief in the manifest destiny and unlimited horizons of the United States and of individual Americans. Like other folk artists in all media, the pottery decorators mirrored the moods of the times.

The technology of stoneware decoration was unlike that of any other decorative craft, for it was entirely dictated and limited by the medium of plastic or dried clay on which the decorators worked. Three essential techniques were used— impressing with a stamp or die in still-plastic clay, incising in semidried clay, and surface glazing, done with a brush or slip-cup quill on thoroughly dried but unfired greenware.

Incising involved scribing or cutting the outlines of a design, and often internal details, too, directly into the still-soft body of a stoneware pot. Incising, too, was time consuming, for it had to be done very deliberately, not only in regard to the placement of lines or cuts but with complete control over the depth and width of each. Variations in pressure on the tools, clay, and in the finished lines could give even the most elaborate design a sloppy appearance.

For obvious reasons, incising as a technique began to disappear in the 1830's and '40's; no pottery could be produced in any quantity if each piece required as much or more time to decorate than initially to make. Incised designs, too, were not applied at all to the majority of pieces; most early stoneware found today is absolutely plain, or has a simple coggled band or a few strokes of blue coloring. Even on decorated pieces, the designs were usually both simple and small in size. Only very rarely were incised designs as large, in relation to the whole piece of pottery, as the later surface-glazed designs. Large, intricate, and imposing incised designs were always unique—such decorations could never feasibly be produced in quantity, and today these are the rarest of all pieces of stoneware. The incised sailing vessels illustrated in Plates 176–179 are examples; perhaps no more than six or eight such illustrated vessels exist. The same is true of other pieces in large proportions —animals, eagles, or human figures.

Once a piece of pottery had been decorated, it was set in the sun or a drying oven from a few hours to a few days. Once dried, the incised designs were then often, but not always, carefully coated or filled with a blue glaze. This could be a glaze brushed on as a fine dry powder and then wiped, leaving only the incised lines filled and colored, and providing very sharp and crisp contrast. More often the entire outlined design was glazed in. Designs which were not subsequently glazed, of course, depended for contrast on the incised lines alone.

Impressing or stamping can hardly be called a decorator's technique, for it was simply a mechanical process. Stamps with small designs in reverse, usually standing in relief, were simply pressed into the newly formed wet pieces, leaving an impression that could look, superficially at least, like very neat incising. If the stamped design was to have its impressed lines colored, the stamp was simply dipped in blue glaze before each impression. Though usually standing alone, stamped designs were sometimes used in combination with hand incising to produce a particularly intricate or difficult small portion of a larger design. It served simply to speed up the process of incising a decoration, and if done neatly did not detract at all from the overall effect.

Stamps, of course, were always used for marking names (though early pieces were commonly unidentified), but decorative stamping is far more common on stoneware of the first half of the 19th century. To be sure, it was used throughout the era of decorated stoneware, but to a far lesser extent as the century progressed.

By 1850 or 1855 the stoneware industry had grown too large and competitive for individual potteries any longer to depend on maintaining a market for bare gray pottery, with incised designs on only a minority of pieces, even for utilitarian use. The new Victorian age, with its great emphasis on sheer quantity of decoration, ultimately even beyond all reason, made essential the use of a new decorative technique that could be applied rapidly yet as elaborately as necessary to every piece of pottery produced. Time-consuming and difficult incising simply could not be speeded up.

Surface-glazed coloring had long been used for simple contrast with the pottery, for filling incised designs, and even for very basic floral designs. Rarely, though, had stoneware decorators ever tried to be artists with glazes, or to paint extensive designs of the caliber of the best incised work. The deep blue glazes which had traditionally been used in coloring stoneware were based on cobalt oxide, one of the four metallic oxides which were then and are still a primary component in ceramic glaze mixtures. Cobalt oxide had several attributes which virtually required its use on stoneware. First, the other metallic glazes, iron oxide for red and some yellows, copper oxide for greens, and manganese for browns and black, proved to be unstable and unpredictable at stoneware-firing temperatures, sometimes resulting in odd colors or patterns, sometimes breaking down completely.

All raw metallic oxides were expensive (in 1836 Nathan Clark was paying thirty-eight cents a pound for his fine-grained "powder blue"). Most were imported from Europe, but fortunately were used in small quantities. As well as its stability, and its quality of blending well with the grays or browns of stoneware, the cost factor was perhaps another prime reason for the universal use of cobalt oxide. Its great strength as a coloring agent made a little go a long way. There were probably as many different specific glaze mixtures as there were potteries using them, but in any mixture only a one or two per cent content of finely ground cobalt oxide would provide a fine royal or deep blue—a greater percentage would result in almost a black. No other oxide could be used effectively at such a small percentage of the whole mixture.

Any glaze required three essential elements—a coloring oxide, a flux that would melt in firing, and a binder that would immediately stick the glaze to the pottery, and prevent it from flowing or dripping once applied. The flux was usually silica—finely ground quartz sand or flint (or sometimes if it was available, borax). For a binder, gum arabic was boiled and dissolved in water, and the liquid was then mixed with the dry components. The resulting glaze could be used as a thick paste or further diluted with water, but it had to be continually remixed, since the coloring oxide and the silica or borax were not readily soluble in water.

The final glaze could be painted on stoneware by one of two instruments, a stiff brush or a slip-cup. Unlike incising in wet clay, the decorator, since he or she was dealing entirely with greenware, could place the pot in any position while working. Brushing left wide flat strokes of glaze, but short ones. All but the most diluted glazes were too thick to flow well from a brush; thus came the need for stiff rather than soft bristles.

The slip-cup was essentially a pottery (earthenware or stoneware) cup with an opening for filling on top and a hollow goose or porcupine quill projecting from a small hole in front. The quill, of varying thickness on different cups, had to be tightly fitted. For quill tracing, the hand-held cup was simply tipped until the glaze flowed through the quill to be traced on the pottery, with the thickness of the traced line depending on both the diameter of the quill and the rapidity with which it was drawn along. When a line was finished, the cup was tipped back. While slip-cups for decorating earthenware plates often had multiple quills, cups for stoneware invariably had but one. The writer has never seen a design on stoneware with the sort of parallel or wavy lines that could have been done with multiple quills.

Brush glazing and quill tracing were far faster than incising, even in large designs, but quill tracing particularly required extreme control of the slip-cup and precise but instantaneous judgment of the width and length of lines. Designs could no longer take the time or be done with the same careful deliberation as earlier.

From 1850 or 1860 to the end of the age of stoneware as an artistic form, what would earlier have been considered elaborate special designs were glazed on the majority of pieces, and the best and most intricate designs, those on large special jugs and fountains, became truly magnificent. Then, between 1880 and 1900 stoneware finally and predictably became a victim of the new technological age. Molded, mass-produced glass became increasingly available at very low cost; pressed and soldered sheet iron and steel products from cans to barrels increased their market and range of uses. First, smaller potteries vanished as the market for stoneware gradually narrowed; others diversified into hotel and restaurant pottery, art pottery, electrical insulators, and numerous other ceramic products. We can well say that stoneware as an artistic form or medium disappeared completely by 1900; crocks and jugs had become mundane products turned out almost entirely by machinery and with no decoration whatsoever.

However impressive their special and most painstaking work may have been, most decorators still earned their day-to-day living and spent most of their time and effort producing a relatively few standard designs. Whether the initial designs were based on the original ideas of the decorators themselves or were required by pottery proprietors is less important than the fact that each decorator developed an individual style—minute characteristics of line, detail, and shaping. Not only standard decorations but particular styles as well were sometimes passed on from teacher to trainee, accounting for a particularly long life span for some designs. The illustrations of the group of very similar birds by William Roberts and the White family of Utica and Binghamton, New York, show what can be deduced from a comparison of numerous examples of the same design produced over a thirty-year period (Plates 34–38, 128, and 143).

One problem inherent in any study of stoneware is the great number of early pieces, and to a far lesser extent later examples, never marked by their makers. Here comparison of designs may be very helpful, for given a single identified piece bearing a strongly individualistic decoration with definite characteristics, it is quite possible to attribute other unmarked pieces to the same maker on a basis of the decorations alone.

Decorators, as they anonymously pursued their craft, drew inspiration from their immediate surroundings—plants and wildlife, agriculture and domestic livestock, and particular sights or events which had impressed them. Each of these various design groupings is explored at greater length in the following chapters.

32. Incising tools were very basic, but since nearly all such instruments were handmade, they occurred in a vast number of different forms. Essentially most were pieces of iron wire or light rod pointed on one or both ends, and with a rough wooden handle attached. Occasionally thin blades or light grooving chisels were used, but generally anything which would scribe a line in soft clay would serve.

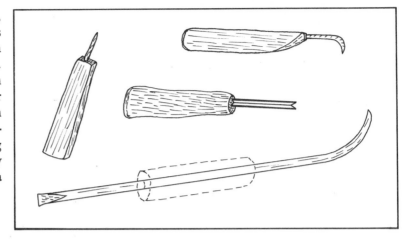

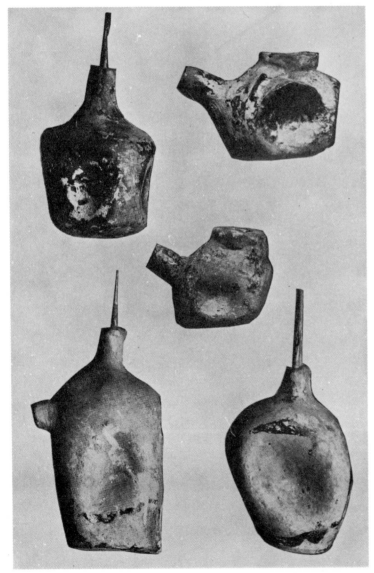

33. Slip-cups were originally used for decorating with slip-colored clay mixed with water to the consistency of light cream. The slip-cup, however, served equally well for tracing lines of oxide glazes. The cup was usually roughly formed of clay (like incising tools probably made by the decorator who used it) with an opening for filling and a small hole for a quill, or a cork or stopper which held a quill. For tracing a line, the cup was simply tipped till glaze flowed through the quill; then it was raised again at the end of a line. Smithsonian Institution.

58

37. Probably dating from the late 1860's or '70's, this five-gallon crock is unmarked, but because of the bird it is obviously from the Roberts or White Pottery. All of the detailed identifying characteristics are clear, in spite of the bird's facing to the left (as did many others on marked pieces). Collection of the author.

38. The same bird design continued into the late 1870's or early '80's but traveled even to the main White Pottery at Utica. The "White's Utica" stamp was the firm's latest marking, under Charles N. White, who succeeded (either son or younger brother) N. A. White. The bird has been somewhat streamlined—probably in the interest of speedy production, but except for internal body details has essentially the same characteristics as the earlier versions; the tail, again fanning in both directions from a central point, harks back to Roberts' pre-1857 version. Did the Whites transfer decorators from Binghamton to Utica, or were decorators sent from Utica for training? We simply cannot tell. Collection of Mr. & Mrs. Walter Luckert.

34. This two-gallon crock, marked "W. Roberts, Binghamton, N.Y.," was made prior to 1857, and bears an early form of William Roberts' standard bird design. The entire decoration was done from a slip-cup; no brushwork is apparent. Note that the tail is a series of separate traces fanning away from a central point, that the head has a comb, the beak is open, the legs are bent, and the body is filled with spots of glaze. The vine on which the bird stands has blossoms done by rapidly swirling the glaze trace in a tight spiral, forming a closed circle. The branches completely bisect the flowers. This was to be the basic form of the bird of Roberts and later Noah White, Jr. until the pottery closed in 1887. Collection of the author.

35. Knowing what the Roberts' bird should be, it seems obvious that this crude effort appearing on a crock of the late 1850's was the work of a completely unskilled decorator, probably a newly hired trainee. The basic characteristics of the standardized bird are apparent—the tail strokes, comb, open beak, bent legs, and spiraled, bisected flower—indicating that William Roberts rather than the actual decorator decided the design. Donald Everhart Winer Museum.

36. Noah White established a pottery in Binghamton adjoining Roberts in 1859 as a subsidiary of his main operation in Utica, New York. The marking, "N. A. White & Co., Binghamton," became current when White's son took over in 1864. With the single exception of the tail strokes, which curve down, this bird is completely similar in all characteristics to the earlier Roberts' versions, leading to one of two possibilities—that White had lured away one of Roberts' trained decorators, or that the two potteries had an agreement to use the same decorators. Collection of the author.

CHAPTER FIVE

Flowers and Leaves

Potteries and individual potters did occasionally make special and unique items of stoneware. Decorators, too, on special order or more likely for their own satisfaction or amusement, sometimes applied elaborate and unusual decorations to single pieces. Still, the typical stoneware pottery was essentially not a craft shop but a small manufacturing business, which depended for its economic existence on sales of standardized and mass-produced pieces by the dozens or hundreds. Hard economic facts, too, governed the decoration of most pottery, and the work of decorators who produced the designs on a piecework basis.

Standardized production of stoneware demanded, first, designs that would attractively alleviate the massive grayness of the pottery yet which could be applied very quickly and often with a minimum of skill. The decorations themselves must have a wide appeal, or at least no great negative appeal, for most potteries offered a rather limited range of designs. Bird or animal designs might be fine in rural areas, but might not sell in cities. Codfish or sea-oriented scenes might do well in coastal areas, but not inland. Even patriotic designs, which would seem to have a universal appeal, in an age of near-violent politics might be nearly unsalable if the mood of a particular area happened to be in opposition to the current president or governor.

Most importantly, however, the more specific designs were also the technically more difficult, and therefore time consuming to produce. Flower and leaf designs thus became the standard—simple, obvious, but unidentifiable flowers, leaves, stalks, and vines could be done minimally with a few scratches of an incising tool or a few passes with a slip-cup brush. So, too, floral designs had no negative appeal, no geographic limits, no real or imagined political significance: in short, they were safe. Stoneware so decorated could be sold to anyone.

Stoneware decoration with specific motifs or pictures, as opposed to simple addition of color, did not really begin until after 1790, but from the beginning general floral designs dominated every other form of decoration. When the practice of incising gradually disappeared between 1825 and 1845 in favor of surface glazing, all designs tended to become both larger and more elaborate, the force of competition outweighing the cost factor. Large and blatant designs were, in fact, as easy to produce as small ones. Floral designs still continued to be the most popular. From observation of existing pieces of stoneware, over a period of time and in different areas, it becomes quite clearly apparent that more stoneware was decorated with floral patterns, by a great margin, than all the other decorative forms combined. Basic mid and late 19th-century crocks and jugs with floral designs, particularly of the simpler variety, are readily available today in virtually any country antique shop; all of the other design forms without exception are at least uncommon; some are extremely rare.

Unlike most other design categories, the floral decorations are usually suggestive rather than intentionally specific. Some are purely symbolic—ropes of brush-stroked leaves, a few brushstrokes in the general form of a flower and stalk, even near abstractions faintly resembling natural vegetation. Many others are clearly flowers, shrubs, or in more elaborate types, whole flower arrangements. Yet the designs are solely in form and not even vaguely identifiable as particular species.

Rather than attempts at renditions in glaze of actual flowers, a number of these designs seem based on what we think of as classic Pennsylvania-German tulips and roses, often seen on early slip and sgraffito-decorated earthenware. In fact, most of these designs are attributable, beyond Pennsylvania, to early German and Swiss earthenware, and to German and Flemish stoneware, which strongly influenced the forms as well as the decoration of all North American stoneware. The wide geographic distribution strongly suggests, however, that the Germanic designs by the 19th century were so commonly accepted and universally known that most decorators never thought of, and probably never even knew, their actual origin.

In examining the entire gamut, we find that a relative minority of floral decorations are even attempts, successful or not, at picturing the actual species of flowers, vines, weed plants, or crops which the decorators found in their own environments. The reasons for this may lie in the fact that thick blue glaze applied with a stiff brush or through a quill is hardly a material lending itself to great artistic precision, nor is clay the material best suited for careful and precise incising. Leaves and flowers, on the other hand, are often rather subtle subjects, requiring more than an outline and a few lines to depict even identifiably, much less adequately. The pottery decorators undoubtedly found that since the twain rarely met with any great satisfaction, it was far more desirable and certainly easier to stick to the realms of imagination and symbolism.

39. Thomas Commeraw, who established a pottery at Coerlears Hook in New York City about 1797, used a basic form of incised floral decoration which typified the late 18th and early 19th century New York City and northern New Jersey makers. Essentially, such designs had smoothly and skillfully incised outlines, but little internal detail, and were then carefully coated with an enamel-like blue cobalt glaze. The marking "Coerlears Hook" was probably applied from a single woodblock stamp. Metropolitan Museum of Art.

40. Another piece, with loop handles perpendicular to the sides of the jar, is marked only "N. York," one of Commeraw's known marks. Even without the mark, however, the leaf and flower design, here in a vertical position, is almost identical to that on the previous piece (Plate 39). Note the figure-eight technique used in incising the rounded bottom-most petals in the blossom. Collection of Mr. John Paul Remensnyder.

41. A third jar, completely unmarked, shows the value of comparing standardized designs to determine attributions to specific makers. The basic silhouette of this piece is similar to the jar marked "N. York," but the design shows precisely the same treatment. The two strokes used to incise each of the lower leaves meet in a slight terminal hook, as on both previous pieces, and figure-eight stroke outlining the rounded petals shows clearly. As a result, this unmarked jar can certainly be attributed to Thomas Commeraw. Collection of Mr. John Paul Remensnyder.

42. This small unmarked jug, *c.* 1800–20, is probably a New York City piece, though the design again has no distinct characteristics from which to identify the maker. Like so many floral designs, the flower is either a composite or purely imaginary. Collection of Mr. John Paul Remensnyder.

64

43. On an unmarked and unidentified jug, *c.* 1800–20, this distinctive flower, with sharp outlines but no detailed internal incising, is typical of early New York–area designs, but is not sufficiently similar to those of any known makers to warrant an attribution. The blossom itself could be based on any one of a number of flowers. Collection of Mr. John Paul Remensnyder.

44. This most unusual design on a New York City crock, *c.* 1800–10, seems to be a flower and stem above a completed separate pattern of leaves. The leaves on the flower's stem, however, sweep not toward, but away from, the blossom. The flower itself is quite similar, even to the lines within the petals, done with a stiff comb-like tool, to at least one other piece by Clarkson Crolius of New York. Oddest of all is the core or pistil of the flower, which appears to be a stamping done with a small die (see Chapter II), while all other outlining is incised. Collection of Mr. John Paul Remensnyder.

45, 46. Both early 19th-century pieces probably by the same (as yet unidentified) maker, this jug and crock bear similar flower designs much like geraniums. The stems and leaves are incised and lightly colored but each of the flowers seem to have been done with two stamping dies, different for each piece. The apparent technique was to do first the outer flowers one at a time by pressing a die to the plastic clay with a rolling motion. Then with a separate stamp pushed directly down, the central blossom was impressed and the overlapping of the outer flowers was erased. Coloring was applied by hand. Small stamped designs were commonly done, but this unusual combination of incising and stamping was one method of speeding up the application of more elaborate designs. Collection of Mr. John Paul Remensnyder.

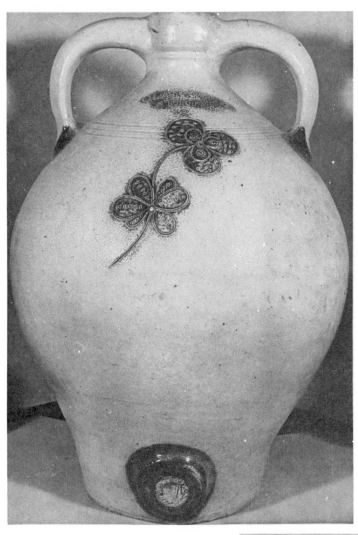

47. Small fountains or coolers, essentially two or three-gallon jugs with spigot holes and often heavy double-loop handles, were commonly used in taverns, particularly in New York State, as containers for and dispensers of wines and brandy. The simple incised plant, possibly a clover, runs over the three bands cut around the jug, and patterns of minute incised cuts add detail to the leaves. The fountain is marked "Clark & Fox / Athens," the partnership which operated the Nathan Clark Pottery of Athens, New York, from 1829 to 1838. Incised designs of any sort are unusual on Clark pieces; the pottery used simple surface-glazed designs almost exclusively from its establishment in 1805. Collection of Mr. John Paul Remensnyder.

48. With no marking, this one-gallon crock is heavier for its size than most stoneware, and has an unusual wide, flat rim. A single flower is carefully incised, including at least the outline of the blossom. The inner petals and pistil are not outline incised, but in shallow relief, possibly stamped with a die, or considering the irregular shape, perhaps roughly sculptured by hand. The internal lines seem to be hand incised. The blue glazing was rather carelessly applied. From comparisons, the maker may have been Jonathan Fenton of Boston, 1794–97. Collection of Mr. John Paul Remensnyder.

49. Holding about three gallons, this unusually large pitcher bears a symmetrical design of two Germanic tulips coming from a central flower-shaped motif. The early 19th-century piece is not marked, but the incised outline and smoothly glazed design indicates that it is probably from a pottery of New York City or New Jersey. The closely spaced but irregular banding at the neck and base was done with an incising tool as the pitcher turned on the wheel, not by coggling. Collection of Mr. John Paul Remensnyder.

50. A three-gallon jug by Williams H. Farrar of Geddes (Onondaga County) New York is marked "W. H. Farrar & Co. / Geddes, N.Y." Farrar established his pottery in 1841, and this is certainly one of his earliest pieces. The sharply and skillfully done tulip design is one of very few presently known examples of incised decoration by an upstate New York maker, (most New York potteries west of Albany and the Hudson River were not established until well after the primary period of incised decorations) and the design itself shows a very definite Pennsylvania-German influence. There is no evidence, however, that Farrar himself had come from southeastern Pennsylvania. Blue glaze was applied thinly to the design; much of the covering salt glaze has flaked or dissolved away. Onondaga County Historical Society, New York.

51. This unmarked crock, judging from its shape and handles, is probably late for an incised design (*c.* 1840–50); very probably it is the product of an upstate New York maker. The silhouette is very similar to other Athens and Albany pieces. The incised design of an inconsistently done plant and two Germanic tulips shows a hesitancy and lack of skill in using the incising tool. Crude slashes have added some detail to the lower but not the upper leaves; the tulips have too many and unequally cut lines. Clearly this was the work of an inexperienced or apprentice decorator. Collection of Mr. John Paul Remensnyder.

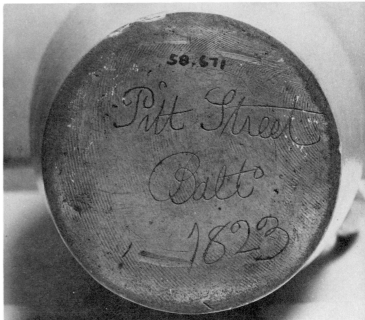

52 a–b. Much stoneware, because of its basic simplicity of form and design, has a certain age-less quality. This pitcher (left), with a design of incised leaves and flowers, could well be a contemporary piece, and is quite striking in the contrast between the very dark blue glaze and the nearly white ground. The wavy line around the lip is a brush applied surface design. The outside of the pitcher is incised in script "Morgan / maker," and base (above) marked "Pitt Street / Balto. / 1823." Thomas Morgan operated in Baltimore, Maryland, from *c.* 1810 to 1837. Henry Francis DuPont Winterthur Museum.

53a–b. This grand fountain with its very Germanic but strangely incised tree is incised on the front "J. W. Smith," and the back is stamped ". . . Smith / Alexa. / D.C." Alexandria, Virginia, however, has not been within the District of Columbia since 1846, when Congress transferred that part of the District west of the Potomac to Virginia. The odd main design is balanced on both sides and the back with three other incised and glazed plants which remind one vaguely of reconstructions of Devonian and Pennsylvanian fossil trees. Around the base the decorator has included small incised versions of other pottery, perhaps standard types which the Smith Pottery produced. One handle and the spigot hole bushing are unfortunately broken. Collection of Mr. John Paul Remensnyder.

54. Madison Woodruff, whose pottery in Cortland, New York, produced this six-gallon double-handled jug, operated for over forty years from 1849. The double handles are rather unusual on late upstate New York pieces. The flower design, here a complete plant done in a blue surface glaze without incising, is again the work of a skilled and specialized hand. The flowers themselves are quite similar to the tulip form so often encountered on Pennsylvania-German pottery. The design shows a confidence of form, and slip-cup quill and brush technique, which could only come from considerable experience in doing the same design over and over again. Cortland County Historical Society.

55. Another unusual piece is this covered jar, almost a classic cookie jar form. The design is an incised plant coming from a pot seemingly made of logs, and the plant itself has terminal twigs laden with berries. Some of the leaves are simply outlined; others to the right have internal incising as well. The blue glazing seems without rhyme or reason; in a few spots leaves have been colored in, in others the glaze surrounds the incising, which is left bare. The separate strip of clay applied above the design is marked "Calvin Whitcom," apparently the recipient. The maker is unknown. Collection of Mr. John Paul Remensnyder.

56. The John Bell Pottery of Waynesboro, Pennsylvania, which operated from 1833 to 1881, became best known for its use of unusual glazes on what we know today as "Shenandoah pottery." The Bell Pottery, however, also produced more standard stoneware pieces, such as this two-gallon pitcher with a granular, bluish body. The decoration of leaves and flowers on all sides is done in brushed blue surface-glaze, and the piece, c. 1850, is marked "John Bell / Waynesboro / 2." Metropolitan Museum of Art.

57. Southern stoneware was only occasionally decorated. Most was left plain, and the 19th-century northeastern practice of turning out increasingly elaborate designs never took hold. This small pitcher, salt glazed over a curious greenish-gray body, is by an unknown South Carolina potter. The decoration is nothing more than a few strokes in blue from a slip-cup, which alone makes the pitcher unusual. Donald Everhart Winer Museum.

58. This four-gallon crock was made at Cornwall, Ontario, 1855–65, and marked "Cornwall / Pottery. C. W. [Canada West]." The design in brushed blue of a bunch of grapes appears as if the sun was shining on it from the top left. The decorator achieved shading by brushing the glaze most heavily on the lower right of each grape and the right of the attached sprig, and only lightly in other areas. It would seem that such a simple and logical technique would be encountered more often, but it is actually rather unusual in stoneware decorations. Collection of the author.

59. Batter jugs, usually holding one gallon, were a specialized stoneware type used to mix and pour pancake batter. Being entirely utilitarian, however, they were virtually always plain or occasionally swabbed with a few strokes of blue glaze around the spout-joint and handles, lacking on this piece. Truly decorated batter jugs are quite rare, no matter what the design. This piece, with very simple but pleasing brushed-glaze flowers, probably dates c. 1840–50. It is somewhat heavier than later and more common batter jugs, and once had a wire bail handle. Collection of Mr. John Paul Remensnyder.

60. The Lyons Pottery at Lyons, New York, produced this one-gallon crock about 1855. The shape is the final vestige of the earlier classical forms, showing that at least at some potteries the new molded, cylindrical form came into being gradually and perhaps reluctantly. The decoration is a simple flowering plant, like all Lyons' floral designs, connected to a central point. Neatly done, the stems and outline of each leaf were done with heavy blue glaze from a quill; the leaves were then filled in with a few brush strokes. Collection of the author.

61. This interpretation of grapes includes an entire section of vine, with the leaves done in closely spaced groups of traces from a heavy slip quill, and the bunch of hanging grapes as an unconnected group of glazed dots. The six-gallon crock was made and marked by "O. L. & A. K. Ballard, / Burlington, Vt.," c. 1860–65, at a pottery which three Ballard brothers apparently purchased from Nichols & Boynton in 1856 and which A. K. Ballard alone sold to F. Woolworth in 1872. The pottery operated until 1895. Shelburne Museum, Inc. Photograph by Einars J. Mengis.

74

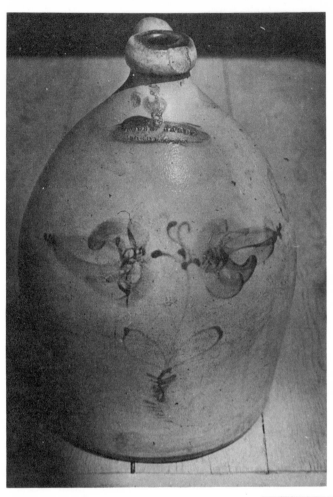

62. The decoration on this Canadian two-gallon jug is in some ways similar to the ever-present Pennsylvania-German tulip design. The fact that, below the simply looped leaves, even roots have been included, is even more suggestive of that origin. Brush strokes of thin glaze have been superimposed, giving the flowers themselves a peculiar transparent quality. The jug, *c.* 1855–60, is marked "F. Eberhardt / Toronto, C. W. [Canada West]," a man who may well have been a Pennsylvania potter who migrated with many other Pennsylvania Germans to western Ontario during the first half of the 19th century. Metropolitan Toronto & Region Conservation Authority.

63. Another one-gallon crock marked "Lyons" is this later cylindrical type, *c.* 1865. The design is more elaborate and sophisticated, probably by a different decorator than that of the piece in Plate 60, and was done entirely with a slip-cup quill. The Lyons Pottery, established as a subsidiary by Nathan Clark of Athens, New York, from 1852, was managed, and after 1867 owned, by Thompson Harrington, who had made stoneware at Hartford, Connecticut before moving to Lyons. In 1872, Harrington was succeeded by Jacob Fisher, who finally bought the pottery from him in 1878. New York State Historical Association.

64. Not only unusual, but a little weird, this surface-glazed design done with a slip-cup appears to be a sprig of some sort of prickly creeping vine. The decorator must have been strangely motivated. The crock is of a form similar to early New Jersey pieces, but unmarked. The painted spirals beneath the handles, however, at least suggest the James Morgan Pottery at Cheesequake, New Jersey (c. 1775–1805) as a possible origin. Collection of Mr. John Paul Remensnyder.

65. Another piece, a five-gallon crock by Eberhardt of Toronto, again shows a definite German influence in its decoration. The flowering plant, coming from the ground or base of the crock, terminates in a blossom divided into quadrants by stems or tendrils, again a design commonly found on Pennsylvania red earthenware. Metropolitan Toronto & Region Conservation Authority.

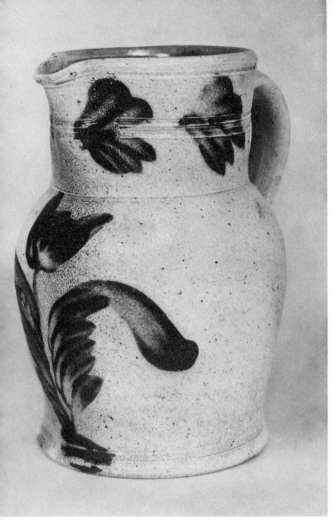

66. A smaller pitcher, with a single large tulip design and additional leaf patterns on the neck, is probably a mid-19th-century Pennsylvania piece. The banding at the neck was done with a three-pronged tool as the pitcher turned on the wheel. There is a short interruption in the banding where the finisher perhaps slackened the pressure on his tool. Henry Francis DuPont Winterthur Museum.

67. In some ways similar to the earlier John Bell of Waynesboro pitcher (Plate 56), this highly decorated but unmarked piece, *c.* 1840, could be from the John Bell Pottery; it is of the same granular, bluish stoneware, and from its shape is almost certainly from Pennsylvania or the middle south. The elaborate flowered vines are entirely surface brushwork. Henry Francis DuPont Winterthur Museum.

68. Low butter crocks are among the least common large stoneware types. This one, of one-gallon capacity, was almost certainly the product of an eastern New York maker, *c.* 1840–45, though it is unmarked and unidentified. The floral design, all brushwork, in a series of sprigs and flowers, runs the full circumference of the crock in two flattened S-curves. Collection of the author.

69. This butter crock, still with its original cover, is somewhat similar in its decoration to the previous piece. Here, however, the leaves come from a thin central stem, and the blossoms are much closer to the traditional Germanic tulip. This piece, too, is probably somewhat later, *c.* 1855–60, with a rounded top, base rim, and unusual handles. Henry Francis DuPont Winterthur Museum.

CHAPTER SIX

Patriotism, Fraternalism, and Miscellany

Patriotic designs, perhaps more than any other category, emerged largely as a manifestation of the effect on the individual of the 19th-century concept of manifest destiny. As previously expressed, however, the stoneware decorator, like other folk artists, was a mirror: on the one hand receiving an impression or image, and at the same time re-expressing that mood according to his own interpretation of it for others. It was in this way that concepts which may first have started as an individual's consciousness and expression, or emanated from decisions of government, by constant reception and reinterpretation became a strong part of the popular American mind.

Like so many popular moods and images, American patriotism of the 19th century was essentially emotional, not pragmatic—the emotional nationalism of a people who had secured their political and social independence in a successful revolution, who had established apparently workable popular government, and who were optimistically and enthusiastically pursuing the

"American dream." It was also, however, the naïve patriotism of a people who had retired from the world stage to concentrate on their own problems and ambitions. It was the patriotism of a people who were (or at least believed they were) in full control of all which bore on their individual and collective destiny, and with a rosy view of that destiny, chose simply to push on toward it.

As the pottery decorators, not unique among folk artists, expressed it, this insulated emotional nationalism was a patriotism of symbols—eagles, the flag, shields, deified national leaders—and of pageants —fourth-of-July parades, band concerts, colorfully uniformed local militia, and national military feats.

In many cases the stoneware decorators lavished their ultimate skills on their eagles and other patriotic designs, spending great time and effort on what was undoubtedly a labor of love rather than of commerce. As labors of love, too, the nationalistic designs on large special pieces are often an excellent

79

indication of the real expertise of individual potters and decorators. Decorative subjects and motifs came and departed, but patriotic designs, particularly eagles, were a favorite subject throughout the century of decorated stoneware, one measure of the enduring strength of this facet of romanticism.

Other forms of stoneware decoration, which defy categorization as actual figures, include both fraternal motifs and other directed designs whose meaning today is lost. Freemasonry in particular was an extremely strong political as well as social force during the early 19th century, a force which was occasionally transcribed by pottery decorators into masonic symbols. Most such symbols encountered today are incised in stoneware of the first half of the century; we find few later surface-glazed examples.

As the "Victorian" age advanced, more and more decorators began at least experimenting with new techniques or adaptations in blue surface glazing, and some as well began producing decorations which were more exercises in pure design than meaningful figures. Perhaps a few potters sought to standardize their work with designs which required no interpretation, but certainly such nonspecific and nonrepresentational decorations are today far less common than would be expected if this had been a general trend. Even to the end of the era of decorated stoneware, the ubiquitous floral motifs and birds continued to be the most popular. Some of the former, however, such as the flowers of the Whites of Utica in chapter five (Plates 70–71, 75), are surely exercises in design whose placement in that chapter is the result more of interpretation than obvious recognition.

Decorations as pure explorations of form and geometric design, however, are quite uncommon, though in simple versions they can be found on very pleasing small pieces (chapter twelve). Others, more elaborate though not necessarily more imaginative, are found only on the larger special and rare pieces. It is rather unfortunate that more decorators did not indulge in these flights of fancy, producing designs that never lose their freshness simply because, in being nonrepresentational, there is nothing about them to be really understood.

70, 71. Sunflowers (or are they poppies?) were a stock design first of William Roberts of Binghamton, New York, and then of his partner and successor, Noah White, whose main operation was located in Utica, New York. The late three-gallon crock in Plate 70 (left), *c.* 1875–80, was slightly bulged, probably by weight being piled on top of it while in the plastic stages of its firing. The flowers are excellently done, obviously by a very experienced decorator. This piece shows unmistakably the same hand which applied the very same sunflower design to William Roberts' stoneware as early as 1855, solid evidence that decorating was a specialized and individual skill in all but the smallest of stoneware potteries. Broome County Historical Society. A similar crock is shown in Plate 71. Collection of the author.

72. This three-gallon jar, with a neck which warped in firing, was made by and marked "S. Skinner & Co. / Picton, C. W. [Canada West]." The unfortunately rather weathered design may well represent a lily, in both quill and brush glazing, though an ear of corn is a possibility too. The leaves were originally outlined in a thicker and denser glaze than that used for filling in. Samuel Skinner operated the Picton Pottery from 1855 to 1867. Metropolitan Toronto & Region Conservation Authority.

73. This three-gallon jug was made and marked by "J. & E. Norton, Bennington, Vt.," c. 1855. As with most sizable pieces bearing elaborate and time-consuming designs, this jug was probably made on special order or at a higher price than ordinary production. The design of a basket of flowers, laid on in heavy blue glaze from a slip-cup, shows no unusual techniques, and is somehow not as pleasing as other designs of the same type. This design is not unique; other identical pieces exist. New York State Historical Association.

74. William Roberts of Binghamton, New York, used occasional strange but simple designs. These stalks, on a jug, *c.* 1865–70, could only be a clump of fiddle-head ferns, new spring shoots which have not yet fully unrolled and developed into leaves. Donald Everhart Winer Museum.

75. Another strange design, this one on a "Whites' / Binghamton" jug, seems to be a pair of chestnut leaves with a stark and bare central twig. Perhaps an exercise, the design does not seem as skillfully done as most Roberts-White decorations. Collection of Mr. & Mrs. Walter Luckert.

76. The Nathan Clark establishment at Athens, New York, was one of the longest-lived potteries in New York State, operating continuously from 1805 to 1900 and producing a great number of unusual, special, and occasionally highly ornate pieces. This two-gallon wine cask, far smaller than most and once with a cover, was first banded with a decorating coggle as it turned on the potter's wheel. The blue-glazed design is not particularly unusual. The spigot mounting, marked "N. Clark, Jr. / Athens, N.Y.," was formed separately in a mold, and then applied to the cask before firing. Nathan Clark, Jr., operated the pottery from 1843 to 1892. New York State Historical Association.

77. This wine or cider cask, unmarked but attributed to Nathan Clark, Jr., is a most unusual piece in that it is completely enclosed, with the top an integral part much like a barrel head. The cooler was filled through the spigot hole. This was probably a trial piece that failed, however, for the lack of any air vent on the top would practically have prevented draining through the tap. The blue design, a long branch or vine covering the entire front half of the cooler, includes brush-applied leaves, tendrils formed by spiraled quill traces, and the flowers or flower pods as groups of closely spaced dots. New York State Historical Association.

78. This three-gallon crock or jar of rather unusual shape is dated 1857, and marked "J. & K. Norton, / Bennington, Vt.," the mark used by the Norton Pottery at Bennington from 1850 to 1861. The date in glaze is quite rare. The elaborate floral wreath, also most unusual, shows signs of the same hand responsible for the heavy Norton basket-of-flowers design, with similarity appearing in the quill-traced loops of the leaves and the unconnected dots representing stems or spikes. Shelburne Museum, Inc. Photograph by Einars J. Mengis.

79. Dated pieces are rare in any period, no matter what the design. This four-gallon crock, made at the Noah White, Jr. Pottery in Utica, is marked "Whites Utica" and dated 1865. The design of a flowering plant, perhaps a rose, has flowers of blue glaze rapidly swirled with the slip-cup quill in small spirals to form closed circles, which are then bisected by the lines which form the stems. This flower is common to pieces of Whites of Utica and Roberts or Whites' of Binghamton, and is reminiscent of similar flowers sometimes found on earthenware plates made by Pennsylvania-German potters. The faded or eroded blue glaze on this piece is an effect of weathering. New York State Historical Association.

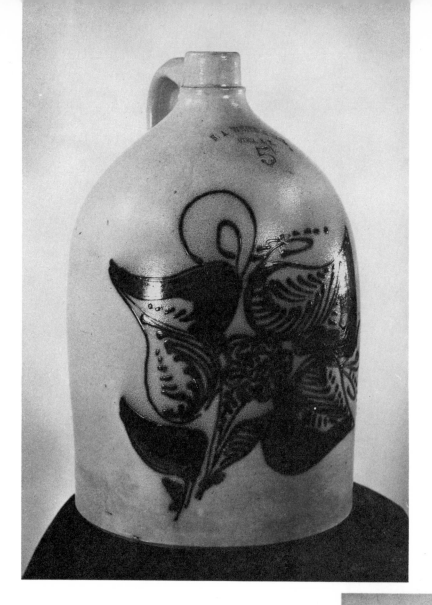

80, 81. The magnificent five-gallon jug in Plate 80 (above), c. 1870–80, is decorated with the most elaborate form of a standard design used by the Noah White firm of Utica, and is marked "N. A. White & Son / Utica, N.Y." The design could be nothing but an orchid with central stem and open petals. It was drawn by rapid but confidently controlled strokes with a slip-cup quill, and a blue glaze so thick that the whole design stands out sharply in relief under the salt glaze. New York State Historical Association. An orchid design on lesser pieces, such as the two gallon crock in Plate 81 marked "Whites Utica," was far less elaborate, but still striking in its sharp heavy lines. Collection of Mr. & Mrs. Richard Weeks.

82. Remarkable for the oddity rather than the quality of its design, this late cylindrical three-gallon jug is marked in blue glaze, "Ithaca, N.Y." and dated 1880. The marking is set off in a wreath of two leafed stems (or perhaps pussy willows) growing from a flowerpot. The piece is not marked, but the maker was probably G. Adley & Co. Donald Everhart Winer Museum.

83. This strange closed blossom on a two-gallon jar, c. 1883, by White & Wood of Binghamton, was done for a reason which cannot be explained, unless it was an unsuccessful attempt at shading. The wide brushstrokes and thin glaze on the left half of the flower and the stem leaves contrast with the quill-drawn dots and swirls of heavy glaze on the right. Broome County Historical Society.

84. This two-gallon jug is typical of southern stoneware, where clays were often more greenish in color than the New Jersey variety, and glazes more varied. The jug, marked "D. H. & Son / Lexington C. H. [Court House] S. C.," is decorated with floral sprigs and script lettering in a white clay slip rather than a metallic oxide glaze. Southern stoneware with even this quantity or quality of decoration is unusual. Donald Everhart Winer Museum.

85. An early Canada West jar, this piece was originally incised with a spray of stems from the rim, terminating in two blossoms near the base. Someone was apparently dissatisfied with this, or didn't notice it, so a new blue-glazed design was then brushed right on over the earlier incising, ignoring it. A most unusual combination. The jar is not marked, but was probably made at the Picton Pottery in the 1850's. Metropolitan Toronto & Region Conservation Authority.

86. With a fine and quite early eagle, this unmarked crock was made probably in New Jersey or Pennsylvania, *c.* 1810–20. The handles are most unusual for this period. The eagle, holding the traditional arrows and olive branch, is incised with extreme care and smoothness of line, with particularly fine detail in the face, lower legs, and the feathered arrows. The lines are filled with blue glaze. Henry Francis DuPont Winterthur Museum.

87. Though not as well executed, this eagle, apparently with the head of a goose, has the flavor of an early 19th-century political cartoon, with the word "Liberty" enclosed in more of a comic balloon than a banner. As well as the arrows and olive branch, the decorator included two crudely drawn American flags. The jug probably dates *c.* 1810–20; the maker is unidentified. Metropolitan Museum of Art.

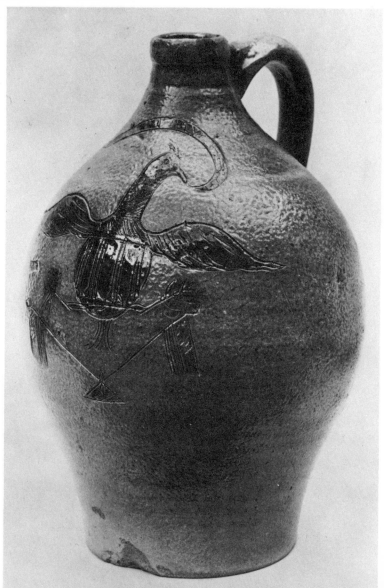

88. Production of eagle decorations seemed to coincide largely with periods of war and national adventures, all stimulating great patriotic fervor. In spite of its crude incising, this eagle with its strange legs and wings, the flying flags, and extended shield stripes, is extremely expressive of the national mood. The unidentified jug is dated 1816, just following the War of 1812 and the year of a successful naval war against Tripoli. Henry Francis DuPont Winterthur Museum.

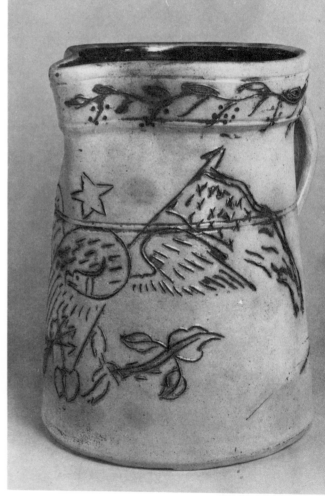

89. Probably a Pennsylvania piece, this pitcher is late for an incised design, dating from the 1840's, and perhaps the Mexican War period (1846–48). The eagle, in deep lines filled with blue glaze, holds arrows and olive branch, and is backed by a flag and topped by a star. The intersecting hearts below the bird are unexplained, and seem incongruous. Henry Francis DuPont Winterthur Museum.

90. Clutching a flag and arrows, this surface-brushed eagle with wings fully spread appears to be flying. Though the flag and arrows may be quill-tracings, the whole bird is a good example of detailed brushwork with a diluted glaze. Weathering has eroded the design. The three-gallon jug is marked "M. & B. Miller / Newport, Pa." and dated c. 1860–70. Henry Francis DuPont Winterthur Museum.

91. This huge sixteen-gallon cooler once dispensed water at William Kelsey's American House hotel, located in Columbus, Ohio, from the late 1830's to about 1860. This grandest American eagle of them all represents the epitome of incised decoration, which was produced in Ohio and the Old Northwest for some years after it had disappeared along the eastern seaboard. The design was done with a very fine stylus, or possibly a needle, so that the artist was able to achieve great precision and detail in the feathers and shield. The maker and decorator are unknown; the markings indicate only the hotel and its proprietor, who most certainly ordered the piece specially made. Ohio Historical Society.

92, 93. As speedy and effective a process as it may have seemed, stenciling never became a common decorative technique—except at the potteries of Greensboro and New Geneva, Pennsylvania, operated primarily by the Boughner and Hamilton families until about 1890–1900. The designs were applied by brushing glaze over a cut stencil held tightly against the side of the crock or jar. Though often elaborate, the Greensboro-New Geneva designs appear flat and obviously mechanical. The two stenciled eagles are among several similar known designs, probably done very late in the 19th century. Henry Francis DuPont Winterthur Museum.

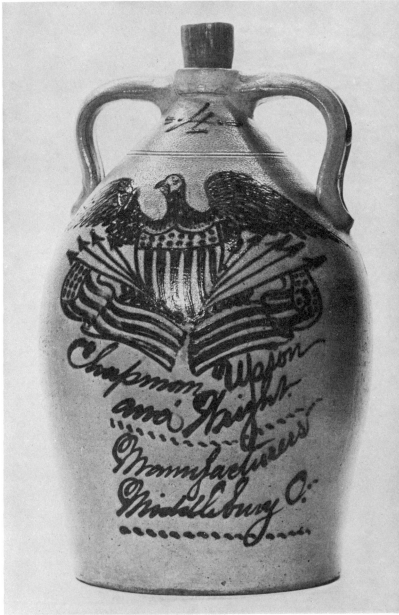

94. This fierce and intense flying eagle, framed in a floral wreath and with a sunburst background, is on a five-gallon crock made by N. A. White & Son of Utica, N.Y. in the 1870's. The word "America" is quill-traced beneath the bird. The manner of forming the two flowers, where the wreath stems cross and by the eagle's tail, is identical to other White and Roberts of Binghamton designs. Collection of Mr. & Mrs. Richard Weeks.

95. Like the huge incised eagle, many of the most magnificent designs are found on pieces of Ohio stoneware. This eagle, emblazoned with shield, and with arrows holding strangely distorted banners, is a bit jingoistic; the olive branches are sandwiched in as an afterthought. The design was done entirely with a slip-cup; no brushwork is apparent. Made probably during the Civil War, the four-gallon double-handled jug is marked in glazed script "Chapman, Upson / and Wright / Manufacturers / Middlebury O.," presumably the makers of the jug rather than of what filled it. Ohio Historical Society.

93

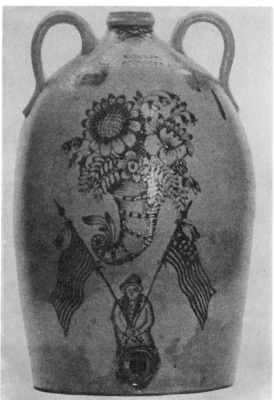

96. This unusual design, like the eagle on the earlier jug dated 1816 (Plate 88), is also crudely executed, though with surprising detail for a design that is so small. The two flags are complete with fringed outer edges; that on the left includes a small eagle in the starred field. Between the flags and the cannon with piles of shot are even tiny crossed drumsticks and a drum. The banded neck of the jug is similar to that on other New York and New Jersey pieces of the early 19th century, but the incised "G. W." marking remains unidentified. Henry Francis Du-Pont Winterthur Museum.

97. Another extremely striking Ohio cooler or fountain, this jug bears a quill-traced man holding two flags and apparently sitting astride the spigot hole at the base. Above him a cornucopia disgorges an intricate flower arrangement, including a finely done sunflower. The cooler is marked "C. Purdy, / Atwater, O.," and dates probably from the 1860's. Ohio Historical Society.

98. Stanley Bosworth of Hartford, Connecticut, who produced this crock in the 1870's, most certainly had more than one decorator in his employ. This design, unfortunately eroded, of two flags on staffs crossed by two swords, is extremely interesting and unusual as a patriotic design, but is hardly a masterpiece of surface glazing. It would be hard to believe that the decorator of this piece was capable of the superb sandpiper and rooster on Bosworth pieces in the next chapter (Plate 135–136). New York State Historical Association.

99. This unmarked crock seems to be an unusual example of a piece that is not Greensboro, Pennsylvania stenciling, for the strongly outlined star and wreath were certainly applied by this method. Though stenciling, other than at Greensboro, was virtually ignored, this unmarked piece in the Shelburne Museum, Inc. is very New England in form, and could certainly be of Vermont origin, c. 1860–80. Shelburne Museum, Inc.

100. A hastily quill-traced shield over two or four swagged banners was evidently a standard design of William E. Warner of West Troy, New York. At least six examples are located, all on similar covered jars. The design, while impressive, is still an example of hasty, hardly careful work. New York State Historical Association. Photograph by Einars J. Mengis.

101. Freemasonry was an important political as well as social movement before the mid-19th century, and a few, though very few, stoneware pieces were produced with designs of Masonic emblems and symbols. This small crock, in form a New York or New Jersey piece, has a crudely incised Masonic divider and tri-square above a hatchet and surmounted by a key, the whole enclosed in an incised ribbon or banner. The design has been colored in blue; the piece is not marked. Henry Francis DuPont Winterthur Museum.

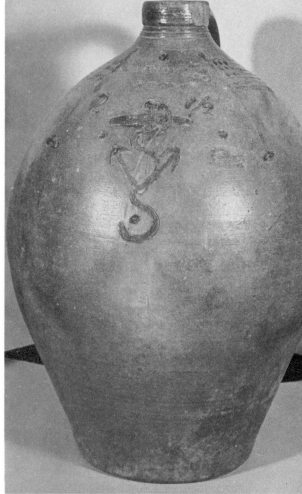

102. Definitely military-oriented designs are far more rare than even general patriotic motifs. This jug, marked "W. Lundy & Co. / Troy" (probably a dealer's stamping), c. 1820–40, bears an incised fouled anchor, the Marine Corps insignia. The anchor is of a form earlier than the jug, with sharply angled hooks and flukes, a wooden cross-stock, and the fouled rope intertwined. On each side are flags flying from vertical staffs, as well as the incised capacity marking, two and a half gallons. The whole design is too lightly incised and glazed to be termed striking. Collection of Mr. John Paul Remensnyder.

103. Another Masonic piece, this jug bears a simple divider and tri-square, colored in blue, over a pyramid. The marking "Goodwin [&] Webster" is that of the partnership of Horace Goodwin and Mack Webster who operated two potteries in Hartford, Connecticut, 1830–40. Collection of Mr. John Paul Rememsnyder.

104. This neatly incised jar was quite likely made as a gift for "P. Darrow of Rome," to whom the piece is inscribed. As well as the incised inscription and the "N. York / 1823" in a border, there are several Masonic motifs, primarily a trowel over a "G." to the left and the square and divider on the right. All incised lines are filled with blue glaze. The jar was made by Justin Campbell, the earliest known maker of Utica, and is marked "J. Campbell / Utica" on the reverse side. New York State Historical Association.

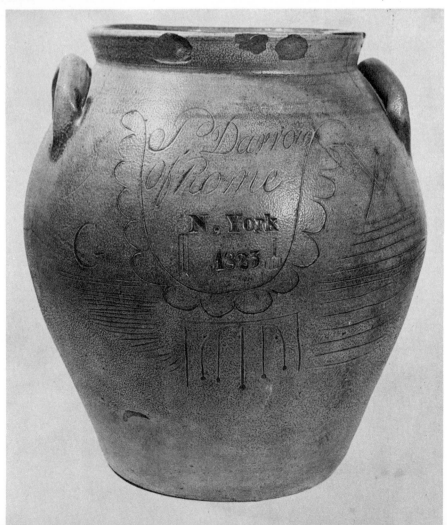

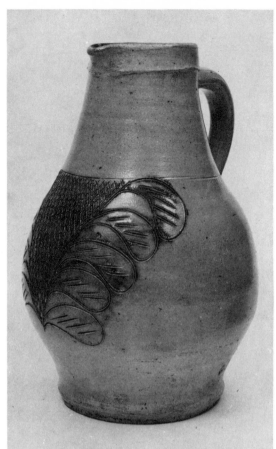

105. The miscellaneous decorations generally defy categorizing; this one particularly so, for it seems to be an example of checkering in the shape of an inverted pyramid. Leaf-like lobes are attached to either side—the checkering could also be meant as the center of a sunflower. With its straight and evenly spaced grooves, the checkering was done with the same sort of tool used today for checkering gunstocks. A two or three-toothed incising tool, with at least one tooth riding in a previously cut line as a guide to each new cut being made, resulting in very even work without a ruler or straightedge. The pitcher, unmarked, is probably from Pennsylvania or Ohio, *c.* 1845–60. Henry Francis DuPont Winterthur Museum.

106. A special and dated piece, this very early jug is inscribed around the circumference "N. Havins 1775. July 18 N. York." The inscription is underlined by four incised floral or leaf-like borders which have been colored with blue glaze like the incised lettering. Beneath one of the borders are the letters "I. C." (not in this photograph), most probably the mark of J. Crolius of New York City, who operated the Crolius family stoneware pottery at Manhattan Wells during the late 18th century. Metropolitan Museum of Art.

107. This design, on a double-handled jar, *c.* 1800, was probably purely imaginative, though it could be based on the British Union Jack. The imprecise incised lines extending beyond the wavy design border, and the sloppily applied and dripped glaze, could make this seem like the work of Paul Cushman of Albany, several of whose pieces are represented in the next chapter. The jar is unmarked, however, and though very likely a New York or Hudson Valley piece, cannot be attributed. Collection of Mr. John Paul Remensnyder.

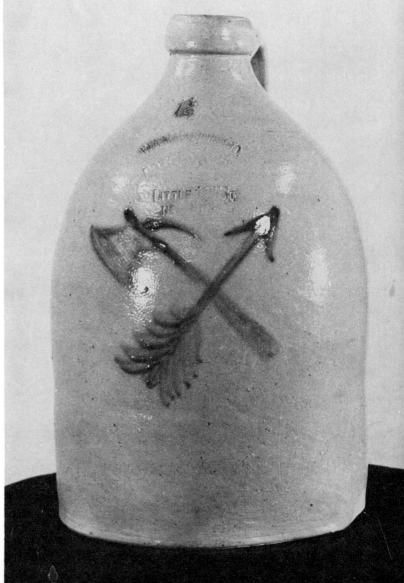

108. This late 19th-century jug by W. A. Macquoid and Co. of New York City bears a simple but very unusual design of a crossed arrow and hatchet—perhaps meant as a tomahawk but looking more like a fireman's axe. Macquoid was known for a number of particularly striking designs; this symbolic creation may have been the insignia of some private organization in New York. New York State Historical Association.

109. One form of common but extremely varied miscellaneous design required a large wholesale order by a purchaser who wanted his own firm's name and address painted in blue slip on his pieces. Sometimes this was combined with other decoration, but typically stood alone. This late 19th-century jug has no maker's mark, but is inscribed in blue script "Wood & Utley / 103 N. Washington / Rome, N.Y." New York State Historical Association.

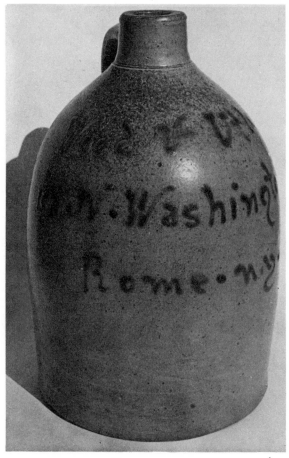

110. Striking in its very simplicity and unusual appearance, this design is nothing more than an imaginative cross formed of eight rapidly quill-traced swirls with a fairly thick glaze. The small one-gallon crock was made by William Roberts of Binghamton, New York about 1855. Collection of Mr. & Mrs. Walter Luckert.

111. Another basic and satisfying example is this nonrepresentational design. Designs such as this graced occasional pieces of the 1860's and later, particularly smaller jugs and crocks which were apparently not deemed worthy of more elaborate work. These lesser designs, well proportioned to small pieces however, are often more pleasing than larger and more complex efforts. This one-gallon crock, made by Madison Woodruff of Cortland, New York, was one of a number of pieces (a collection of her own work) from the estate of a woman who worked as a decorator for Woodruff in the 1880's. New York State Historical Association.

112. Decorators at the Norton Pottery in Bennington, Vermont, had an obvious taste and flair for rococo swirls and heavy spots, as in this quite elaborate design. The six-pointed star was formed of many short lines from a slip-cup, drawn from the outside toward the center, so that each line flowed from a globular beginning to a thin point. The origin of this strange technique cannot be established, but in stoneware decoration, at least, it was perhaps first used at the Norton Potteries at Bennington, Vermont. This jug, marked "J. & E. Norton," was made between 1850–59. New York State Historical Association.

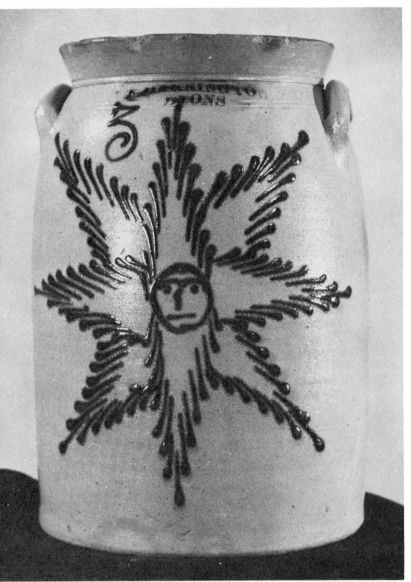

113. Made by Thomas Harrington at Lyons, New York, before 1867, this eight-pointed star, or sunburst, with a face in the center almost jumps out from a three-gallon jar. The design technique is identical to (though the actual motif is far different), and could be contemporary with, the previous piece (Plate 112). Harrington's later large-lettered marking suggests the 1860's. New York State Historical Association.

114. This four-gallon crock from the 1870's marked "J. M. Burney / & Sons / Jordan," (near Syracuse, New York) is yet a further example of how an unusual decorative technique could become widely accepted, but be greatly modified by different individual decorators. This four-pointed star, like Harrington's earlier design with a face in the center, was certainly based on observation, not innovation. Onondaga County Historical Society.

CHAPTER SEVEN

Birds

People have always been fascinated by birds, not only for what they are but for what they can do, how they behave, and how they live. Beyond the domestic birds, we have in our environment hundreds of wild species, from songbirds to eagles, some colorful, some drab, some with strange ways or eating habits, and many which mysteriously migrate twice a year. Great numbers of bird watchers and winter bird feeders, the membership of conservation organizations, and wildlife periodicals all attest to the great public interest that birds engender. Of all the forms of life around us, birds have by far the greatest following of students and protectors. This has probably always been true. In fact, a century ago, when the birds' monopoly of flight was still unbroken and our knowledge of biology was only beginning to accumulate, birds must often have appeared as wondrous creatures indeed.

Mystified and fascinated must have been the pottery decorators as well. Of all the many forms of animal life that were applied as decorations to stoneware, birds predominated in both variety and number. In fact, from the comparative quantity of existing pieces, far more bird designs were produced than all other animal forms combined. Though many pottery establishments and individual decorators generally concentrated on a few stock and standardized designs that could be done very rapidly but very skillfully by experienced hands—which invariably meant floral designs—it would also seem that virtually every decorator at one time or another did at least a few birds, for bird designs appear at least occasionally on pieces bearing the mark of nearly every notable 19th-century stoneware pottery. This alone, if nothing else, would account for the great existing variety.

Some potteries, even those which were sizable operations over a considerable time span, such as the Clarks of Athens or W. H. Farrar of Geddes, New York, apparently did very few bird designs. Birds were not particularly an easy form for an unskilled or inexperienced decorator in incise or glaze, usually entirely freehand, and the bird designs of decorators who did one only occasionally are often, like much of what we term folk art, rather crude in technique and execution. This technical crudity, however, often enhanced the decorator's basic intents and concepts, so that some of the crudely drawn birds can at the same time be the most appealing.

The most remarkable bird designs came from potteries or areas known today for large numbers of such designs—the town of Fort Edward, New York, the home of at least four different potteries where decorators apparently served an area rather than a particular establishment; Roberts of Binghamton and the Whites of Utica, who merged operations and quite obviously trained decorators in both cities to produce a standard bird design; Stanley B. Bosworth of Hartford, Connecticut, and others.

Most decorators, guided and limited to a considerable extent by the materials with which they worked, when doing bird designs on stoneware produced either completely imaginary creatures or composites of familiar species. A design might include some characteristics of a sparrow, a robin, and a pigeon, all in combination, but, of course, the result is not identifiable as any particular bird.

The identity of others, rendered with a good deal of decorator's license, can usually be guessed at. In spite of conflicting features, particularly notable characteristics will often imply the bird the decorator intended.

Some birds, often the best done technically, were so faithfully and well executed, even accounting for the limitations of thick glazes, stiff brushes, and slip-cup quills, as to be readily identified. Chickens and peafowl, robins, sparrows, shore birds, and wood birds all appear as the species most familiar to the decorators. Exotic birds appear as well, however, in spite of the doubtful presence of many such birds in 19th-century North America. Perhaps, like fanciful designs of exotic animals, bird designs came from illustrated books, from models belonging to traveling circuses, or the country's few existing zoos.

The variation of bird designs, both incised and in surface glazes, is so great that it would be entirely possible to study and specialize in the ornithology of stoneware alone. To say nothing of composites and pure imagination, the range of identifiable bird designs alone is very great. The bird designs, too, are perhaps more often than other design forms of a very high technical quality, well formed, sharp in line, and crisp in detail—designs of which the decorators could be proud. Particularly in the later surface-glazed designs, the birds are often of large size as well, which gives sizable jugs or crocks a near grandeur.

115. Either an eagle or a pigeon, this shifty-eyed bird with wings, breast, and tail very lightly glazed in blue, decorates a jug by Israel Seymour of Troy, New York. The marking "I. Seymour & Co." means probably that the jug was produced in 1824 during an abortive partnership; except for this short period Seymour used only his individual name in markings from 1809 to 1852. The naïve bird was apparently incised by someone who had never seen an eagle, or was not on familiar terms with any pigeons. Collection of Mr. John Paul Remensnyder.

116. With its heavy wings and regal head, this bird is probably an eagle, perched in a rather impossible position. The bird's form and the incising is rather crude, quite obviously the work of someone unskilled at decorating. The leafed stalk extends, with an abrupt change on the left to a different technique and leaf type, to form a wreath around the marking "Boston" just above the eagle's head. The maker of this jug, Jonathan Fenton, came to Boston in 1794 and established a pottery, but found New Jersey clay too expensive. In 1796 he moved on to New Hampshire. His sons later established the great Fenton potteries at Bennington. Henry Francis DuPont Winterthur Museum.

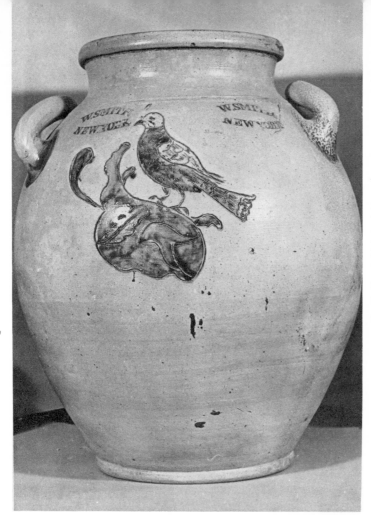

117. New York City has apparently always had its population of pigeons, as this neatly incised but realistically bedraggled bird can attest. The lump of whatever it may be on which the pigeon is standing, from the deliberate outlining, obviously had some specific intent which is beyond present understanding. The bird's body and tail were blue glazed; the head and wings were not. The "W. Smith / New York" marking refers to Washington Smith, who operated the Greenwich Pottery from 1834 to 1850. Collection of Mr. John Paul Remensnyder.

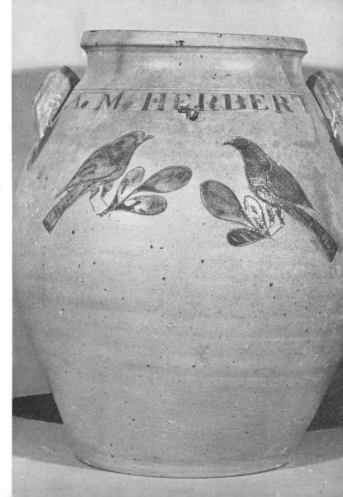

118. This jar, the handles of which are dated *c.* 1830–40, which is late for an incised piece, is marked "A. M. Herbert" in incised lettering, though the maker is not indicated. The two incised birds, facing each other, are well, but simply, outlined and colored, with a few neatly placed cuts adding detail to the leaves and the bird's tails. There is some similarity in treatment of the birds on this jar and the one on the previous piece (Plate 117), but this was made by Nicholas van Winkle of Herbertsville, N.J. (*c.* 1820–40). Collection of Mr. John Paul Remensnyder.

119. This pigeon bears out an interesting but usually insupportable theory—that decorators, probably inexperienced in freehand work, did sometimes sketch out their designs on the clay before incising. Note that the bird, competently but not unusually well done, has what seems to be a double image to the right of the head and breast, a double beak, and an extra leg and claw under the glaze. All this was the results of a preliminary sketch drawn with a pencil or light stylus that left impressions in the clay. The crock itself dates *c.* 1810–25 but is unmarked. Collection of Mr. John Paul Remensnyder.

120. Though the crock, by its handles, is probably somewhat later, *c.* 1825–30, this outline-incised pigeon is quite similar in its silhouette and general treatment to that on the previous piece (Plate 119). The bird is also a little more confidently and smoothly done, this time without apparent preliminary sketching. This crock is almost identical in shape to the earlier piece, and like it, unmarked. Collection of Mr. John Paul Remensnyder.

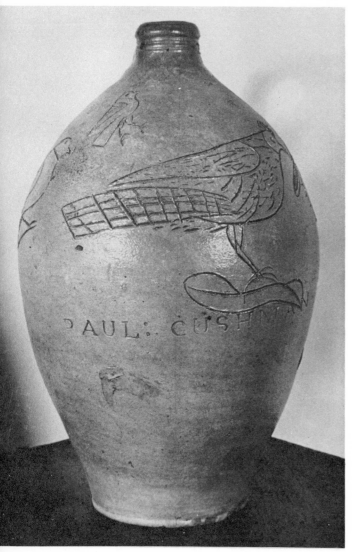

121. Paul Cushman, one of the earliest stoneware potters in Albany, New York, made this jug (*c.* 1810–20) marked simply "Paul: Cushman." Though Cushman was a reasonably good potter, the incised designs on his stoneware always seem extremely primitive, for example the one large and two small birds sculptured into the surface of this piece. No blue glaze was used to fill the lines; the heaviness of the stylus cuts alone provides sufficient contrast under the covering salt glaze. The rolled and banded neck of this jug, like those on jugs by Daniel Goodale of Hartford and early New York makers, is very similar to earlier German and English designs. Albany Institute of History & Art.

122. Another Paul Cushman piece, a cooler with a deep dent in the left side from some drying rack or kiln accident, is again indicative of his crude workmanship. The incised bird with its projecting tail, crest, and short triangular beak seems to be a blue jay. The fish are unidentifiable. As well as the careless application of glaze, the formed barrel banding is uneven, shaped by an unsteady hand on a wheel revolving too slowly. Albany Institute of History & Art.

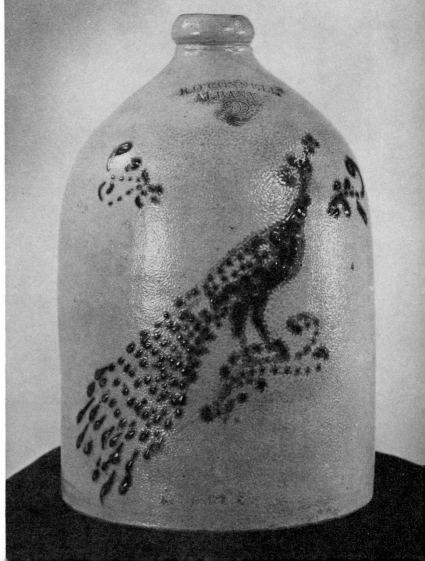

123. This wine or brandy fountain jug with double loop-handles was made by Paul Cushman of Albany, c. 1815–25, and marked "Paul: Cushman" above the spigot hole. Though one of Cushman's more elaborate existing pieces, the decorations as usual appear hastily done and rather crude. This jug may have been a facetious or humorous wedding present. Certainly the two birds, the long-tailed one on the left, obviously the male with dishonorable intentions, and the hearts have some long-lost meaning, as probably did the other designs. Blue glaze was painted, almost slopped, on the designs and the cooler in an uneven fashion, so that it gives the whole piece a rather confused appearance. Albany Institute of History & Art.

124. Peafowl were often kept on 19th-century farms, serving both as feathered watchdogs, for they make a penetrating and unforgettable sound, and as eliminators of insects and grubs. The peacock, one of the most striking and colorful of all birds, stands regally surface-glazed on this two-gallon jug marked "R. O'Connell / Albany." Done entirely in spots and traces of blue glaze so thick that the design stands out in relief, the bird is unfortunately somewhat weathered. New York State Historical Association.

125. This bird chasing a fish seems perfectly content to stand woodenly by while its prey escapes. The figures of both bird and fish are very simply outline-incised, and show no great artistic skill, but the scene itself is quite unusual. The covering salt glaze became mottled in firing. The unmarked jug, c. 1830–40, was not very carefully finished; the marks of the coiled clay still show very clearly. Collection of Mr. John Paul Remensnyder.

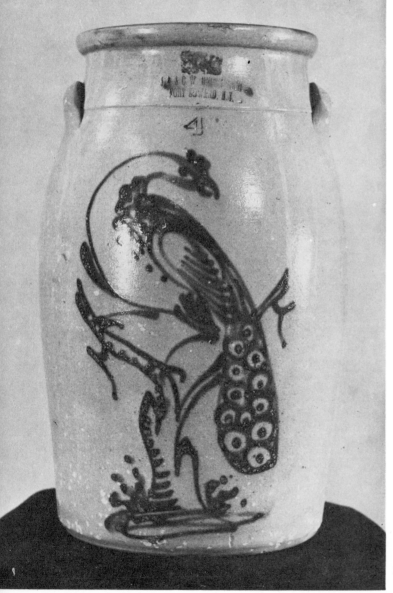

126. An elaborately applied and magnificent peacock, standing in a bush and giving voice, fills the side of this tall four-gallon jar marked "J. A. & C. W. Underwood / Fort Edward, N.Y.," c. 1860–75. Like that on the O'Connell jug (Plate 124), this peacock was done entirely with surface quill-tracing, again in a thick glaze which stands in relief. While simple bird designs are not uncommonly found even today, large pieces bearing grand and elaborate animals such as this are quite rare. New York State Historical Association.

127. Doves of peace, which these birds appear to be, contesting for position on an olive branch, make an unusual design. The birds are very neatly incised, with the depth and width of the cuts creating and controlling the feathers and shading; the design itself has no blue glaze. The bands on the eight-gallon wine or cider cask were formed as the raw piece turned on the wheel, somewhat similar in treatment to Paul Cushman's Albany pieces, though far more skillfully done. The blue glaze was then applied with a brush. The cask was made and marked by "Amos Seavey / Chelsea," Massachusetts, c. 1850. Henry Francis DuPont Winterthur Museum.

128. Fountains of this quality were very unusual products of upstate New York potteries. The maker, Thomas Harrington of Lyons, was an experienced potter who had come from Hartford in 1852. With its banded and colored base and rim and rope-twisted handles, the fountain is finely proportioned and balanced; yet it is simple, avoiding the Victorian age's more rococo influences. The carefully surface-glazed bird, perhaps a grouse, sits on a resprouting tree stump, an appropriate but most unusual background. The shading, which is even more unusual, was applied from a quill as a series of lines in the manner of a draftsman or engraver rather than a painter. Collection of Mr. John Paul Remensnyder.

129. This rather grotesque and unhappy-looking bird and the plant it stands on were incised and glazed in blue, with filled lines. The two-gallon jar is an early 19th-century piece, unmarked and by an unidentified maker. The strongly outlined and heavily incised flower, contrasted with the more lightly and crudely done bird whose tail overlaps a leaf, leads to reasonable speculation as to whether this design shows two different hands —one decorator who did the flower, and another who then added the bird. Collection of Mr. John Paul Remensnyder.

130. The typical bird of William Roberts of Binghamton was a full-breasted one with a prominent beak, rounded wings, and tail feathers done as a series of long and separate strokes with a slip-cup. Purely imaginary creatures, the Roberts and later Noah White birds at their best depended on great skill and, above all, long experience on the part of the decorator. Rather than the usual flowered vine, this bird is sitting on a sprig of curled leaves, evidently by the same hand as the Roberts fiddlehead fern design (Plate 74). New York State Historical Association.

131. Finely incised and colored, this sparkling sharp-eyed bird bears a striking resemblance in the treatment of head and beak to that on the previous and probably much earlier piece (Plate 129), though the jars themselves are not similar. This bird is by far the more precisely and competently done, on an unidentified piece, c. 1840–50. Comparison of the two offers at least the impression that the later bird could well be by the same but now more skilled decorator who, as an apprentice or with certainly far less experience, incised the earlier version. Collection of Mr. John Paul Remensnyder.

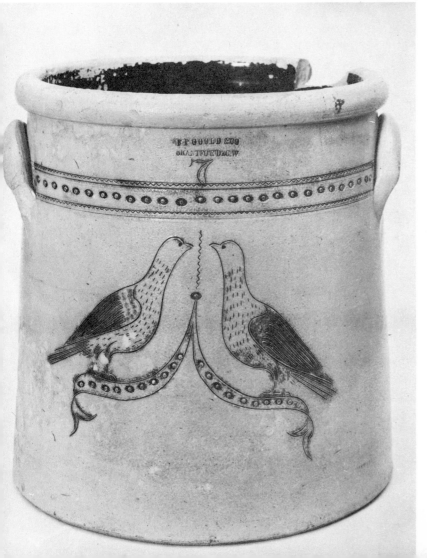

132. Incised motifs in any form are rare on Canadian stoneware, since no Canadian stoneware potteries operated much before 1850. This pair of crisply but simply incised birds is one of the finest examples to come to light, and the crock is one of the latest known incised pieces. In the forward curve of the leading edges of the wings and the rendering of heads and beaks, the birds are very similar in treatment to earlier New York State forms. The incised lines and wing surfaces are blue glazed. In the banner and within the coggled band, a stamped elliptical rosette is used extensively. The crock is marked "F. P. Goold & Co. / Brantford, C. W." Franklin Goold, who is known for other finely decorated pieces, operated the Brantford, Ontario, pottery from about 1862 to 1867, and came originally to Brantford from Hawleyton, New York. Collection of Dr. & Mrs. William McGill.

113

133. Domestic birds such as the ubiquitous chicken often appear in a characteristic activity, which with chickens seems to be eating. This sharply and neatly surface-glazed bird, on a four-gallon churn marked "New York / Stoneware Company / Fort Edward, N.Y.," is a combination of slip-cup strokes in the body and brush strokes in the wing and tail feathers. The open-beaked chicken is quite obviously after a few kernels of corn. The New York Stoneware Company operated from about 1870 until after 1890. New York State Historical Association.

134. Another chicken, on an unmarked two-gallon crock, c. 1870–80, of New York State origin, like that on the churn (Plate 133) is almost identically engaged in eating corn, but was glazed by a different hand. With a perhaps more realistic and chicken-like comb and tail, this bird shows the unfortunate effects of long weathering—a slow dissolution of the glazes. Collection of the author.

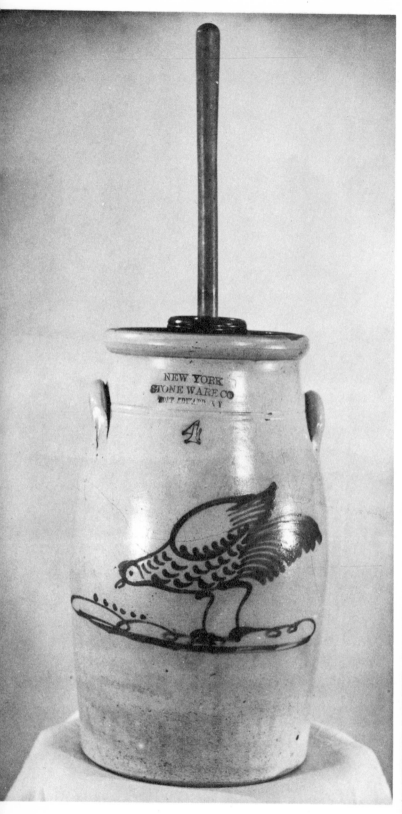

114

135. Just as the chicken's characteristic pose is eating, the rooster's is preening, with comb rigid and tail feathers extended. This bird, all in brushed glaze, is on a late 19th-century five-gallon crock marked "S. B. Bosworth / Hartford, Ct." Old Sturbridge Village.

136. Standing on one leg, this unusual bird on a two-gallon jar, *c.* 1870–80 by S. B. Bosworth of Hartford, could only be a spotted sandpiper, the most common of American shore and marsh birds. The scene is further reinforced by the two brushed-on lower plants and, to the left of the bird, a marsh cattail. Stanley Bosworth, or his decorator, had far more technical and artistic skill than most. Old Sturbridge Village.

137. Almost a rococo bird, this noble creature was incised in much greater detail than most, with fringes of feathers and carefully handled, quite elaborate wings and tail. The plant, framing a patch of ground on which the bird stands, includes even roots at its base, another Pennsylvania-German influence found on earthenware pottery and occasionally in furniture inlays. The bird is even more striking, though probably not intentionally so, because the overlying salt glaze became severely balled and mottled from a rapid temperature drop during firing. The pitcher is unmarked, but its form is early, *c.* 1800–20. Collection of Mr. John Paul Remensnyder.

138. Perched on a fence and apparently crowing, this bird was perhaps meant to be a rooster, though the similarity is hardly convincing. A unified surface-glazed scene such as this, with the ground and grass, the fence, and the bird as the focal point is most unusual. The five-gallon jug is marked "West Troy Pottery." New York State Historical Association.

139. This regal bird, probably intended as an eagle, was traced from a slip-cup in the same thick dark glaze that characterizes so many bird and animal designs. The bird is superficially very similar to that in Plate 137, though not by the same maker. Laid down in thin separate lines, the glaze flowed together to form the solid portions of the wings and tail, and the entire design stands out in relief. The four-gallon crock, c. 1860–70, is the product of a so far unidentified Albany maker, possibly R. O'Connell, a late maker who did the earlier peacock design (Plate 124). New York State Historical Association.

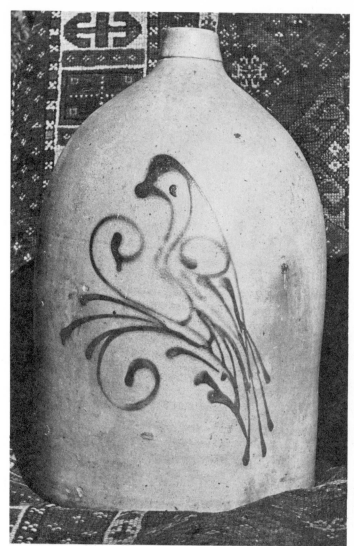

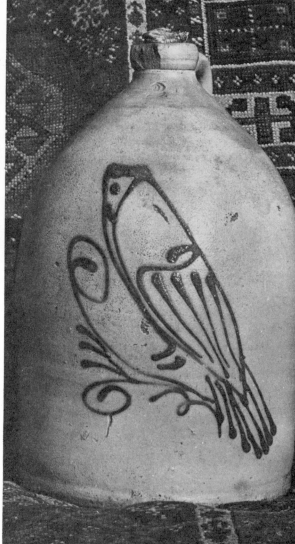

140, 141. These simple and rapidly traced birds grace two Canadian jugs very obviously from the same pottery, and dating *c.* 1860–70, though neither is marked. The birds, though they vary as any completely freehand work must, are by a single decorator. The jugs, though found in southwestern Quebec, are products of the Cornwall Pottery at Cornwall, Ontario, and the birds are typical of this pottery. Collection of Mr. William Snavely.

142. With its small blue quill-traced bird, a good example of those done at Picton, Ontario, this three-gallon crock was made sometime during 1867–1879, the period when George Lazier, the founder Samuel Hart's son-in-law, managed the Hart Pottery. The bird is very similar to others decorating late 19th-century pieces from several New York State potteries, to be expected since both Samuel and William Hart, who established the pottery in 1849, trained in and came from New York. Royal Ontario Museum.

143. Another similar crock, also of the 1870's, bears a still different bird, and a Quebec merchant's mark, "Fortin & Morency / Marchand Epiciers / Coin Des Rues Lous / Le Fort & St. Pierre." Like the universal cylindrical crock, the bird in its treatment shows no great divergence from other standardized glazed birds of the late stoneware period, no matter what their origin. The maker of this piece may well have been the St. John's Pottery at St. John, Quebec. Royal Ontario Museum.

144. Extremely elaborate pieces, such as this five-gallon double-handled jug marked "Whites' Utica," were virtually always specially made. The jug has the date of 1864. The two birds, of uncertain identity but perhaps birds of paradise, were first well located and balanced, probably by lightly sketching on the dry clay. The glazing in thick blue was then very precisely done from a slip-cup with a fine quill to achieve the thin fine lines. Certainly by one of the White pottery decorators, the birds, in the treatment of heads, beaks, and tails, are very similar to the more usual White and Roberts bird designs. New York State Historical Association.

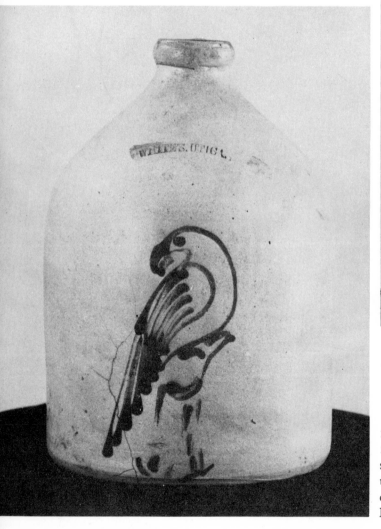

145. It is difficult to accept a tropical flamingo on a late 19th-century jug marked "Whites of Utica," but the resemblance is strong. In fact, though, the identity of this unusual but hastily glazed bird is quite uncertain, and the design has also lost detail by weathering. New York State Historical Association.

146. By the 1890's, when the West Troy Pottery produced this three-gallon crock, stoneware had become entirely an industrial product—as an example of the potters' craft it had been in decline since the 1860's. Decoration, too, became generally more routine and less skilled and imaginative—an assembly line operation. This bird, done in the last days of decorative stoneware, shows signs of being glazed by a skilled decorator, but one who simply had too many pieces to do in too little time. As on many very late 19th-century pieces, the design was hurriedly and carelessly applied. Shelburne Museum, Inc. Photograph by Einars J. Mengis.

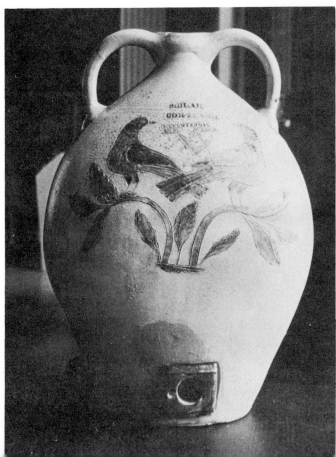

147. This double-handled serving jug with spigot bushing is yet another example of two incised birds in a symmetrical setting, but here the birds are surmounted by a Masonic symbol and the small stamped legend, "Anti-masonic Forever." The jug is marked by Sylvester Blair, Cortland, New York, 1829–35. Henry Ford Museum.

121

148. With incising as sharp in detail as copperplate engraving, this jar with a domed cover is decorated with neatly leaved twigs, possibly willow, and a pigeon-like bird enjoying a few seeds. Below, quite unrelated to the pastoral bird, a bristly fish of mean disposition is about to gobble a meal. The jar, marked "T. Whiteman," and on the reverse side "1853," is a piece of rare quality, and probably from New Jersey or southern Pennsylvania. Whiteman was probably the recipient, not the maker. The reverse of the jar, with a raised applied eagle design, is illustrated in Plate 191. Henry Francis DuPont Winterthur Museum.

149. As a transition to the next section, no piece could be more adequate than this scene of what appears to be a tuna with a broad and silly grin, in the clutches of a stony-faced kingfisher. Though not elaborate or even unusual in skillful incising or glaze, this picture is still one of the most charming, humorous, and ridiculous to be found on any stoneware. The large crock, dating from *c.* 1830, is unfortunately not marked, though it is very probably a New York State piece. Collection of Mr. John Paul Remensnyder.

CHAPTER EIGHT

Animals, Land and Water

Perhaps the most appealing of all the designs found in endless variety on stoneware are pictures of animals. Nineteenth-century America depended on animals—horses for transportation; cows for milk, cream, and butter in an age long before dairies existed or milk came to the door in bottles; chickens for eggs; and pigs for pork, ham, bacon, sausage, and the only cooking fat, lard. Even in the largest cities most people were quite familiar with domestic and farm animals, certainly far more people than would be today. Horse stables also housed cows, and even chickens were common, away from the main thoroughfares.

Rural America, from the outskirts of cities to the distant frontiers, was essentially agricultural in spite of the increasing influence of small individual or entrepreneurial crafts and industries. Rural villages, first established on the line of the ever Westward-moving frontier, existed primarily as support units, with their stores and craft enterprises, and as marketing centers for surrounding agricultural areas.

With their dependence on domestic animals for everything from transportation to food, agricultural areas were, if anything, animal-dominated societies, though hardly more so than the cities. Added to this was the fact that on the too-often subsistence level farms and in the villages, wild animals—deer, rabbits, squirrels, as well as fish—were an important supplementary source of food. For many people fall hunting was too much of a necessity to be considered a sport.

Pottery decorators, who very often rendered designs of animals with complete personalities rather than as mere forms, were products of the areas in which they worked. They knew not only the anatomy and physical characteristics but also the moods, vagaries, and vicissitudes of those animals on which everyone's existence and comfort depended. Thus they were able to express on clay, with stylus and incising tools, thick glaze, slip-cup, and stiff brush, these most ordinary animals as they knew and saw them. The decorators, though, did most fanciful designs of exotic animals as well, animals they might have occasion to see once or twice, but with which they could never really become acquainted. And so, in their renditions of the less familiar creatures, the pottery decorators implied and added the personalities of the animals of their own environment, with often startling and humorous results.

Even in the most isolated areas people, who themselves might never in their lifetimes travel a hundred miles from their birthplaces, were beginning to develop an awareness that other and strange environments and cultures existed and a naïve knowledge of the distant corners of the earth. Children in school used heavily illustrated geography books published in great numbers and filled with errors and misconceptions. Still in an age with at best a paucity of illustrated reading matter, adults too poured over these books with their crude maps and wood engravings of strange places, people, and beasts.

Perhaps the strongest influence, however, was the circus and its colorful literature. During the late 19th century, and particularly after the Civil War, small traveling circuses and carnivals were always preceded at any stop by lurid posters and handbills. Circuses brought the wonders of the earth and animals no one had ever seen before to the people no matter where they were.

The influence and excitement of the unfamiliar and exotic was no more lost on the pottery decorators than it was on artists in other media—folk painters, furniture makers, rural carpenters. Look, for example, at the much delayed effect of European styles on folk furniture or the Greek, Roman, and Gothic revivals on rural architecture. The further in time and distance the exotic influence was removed, however, the more subject to interpretation and pragmatic change it became; this, too, extended to all fields.

Little did it matter that fish had most expressive faces, that lions sported leopard spots and wide grins, or that familiar deer were zebra striped. The stoneware decorators painted animals quite obviously for their own pleasure and amusement; in a period before the union mind had replaced creativity it made no difference to the artist that the piece being decorated might be a special order for a customer. (It also well might have been the decorator's own.) As with all good things, however, the imaginative animal decorations required time and thought. When a pottery had to produce in quantity to survive, however, and the decorator most probably did glazed designs on a piecework basis, except during slack periods or when the customer was paying, there was little time to be spent in conceiving elaborate designs. Thus animals on stoneware were never done in any great quantity, and in spite of a probably higher than normal survival rate because of their extreme appeal, are today among the least common designs.

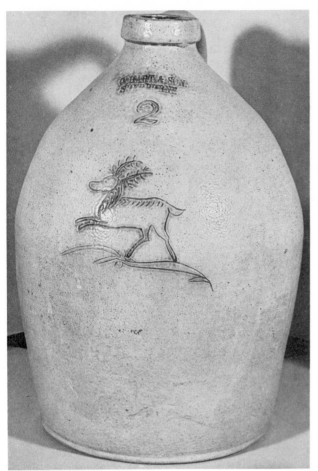

150. What better a design for Charles Hart of Sherburne, New York, than an incised hart, that European cousin of the North American caribou. This neatly incised animal, with the lines filled with blue, may have been intended as a standard design, but it is in fact one of very few examples of incised designs by this pottery, and by far the latest of any known incised designs dating after 1866. James Hart came to Sherburne in 1841 with his son Charles, who succeeded to the pottery and took his own son into partnership as C. Hart & Son in 1866. Collection of Mr. John Paul Remensnyder.

151. One of several animals done with evident regularity at the Norton potteries of Bennington, Vermont, was a surface-glazed deer, which on every observed example was characterized by some degree of a zebra-stripped body. Each scene, too, included a post and rail fence, usually to the left of the animal. The designs, like the birds of Binghamton and Utica, were probably instigated by the proprietors rather than the decorators. This two-gallon crock, marked "J. & E. Norton," was made in the 1850's. Henry Francis DuPont Winterthur Museum.

152. Another truly grand piece and covered with a full forest scene, this water fountain marked "Fort Edward / Pottery Co." at Fort Edward, New York, shows some evidence that a Bennington decorator may have been enticed away. The deer—there are three showing and three others on the reverse side—have full zebra stripes, and some have spots as well. The scene too includes the ubiquitous fence section on the left, as well as a spruce tree very similar to that on the previous piece (Plate 151). Like all such fountains, this piece was produced for a special order, probably in the 1860's. New York State Historical Association.

153. As both domestic and as wild animals, rabbits appeared on stoneware in varied poses. Children have called this an Easter bunny in his nest, though it is simply a rabbit hiding in a rococo underbrush. William E. Warner of West Troy, New York, produced the crock in the 1860's or '70's. New York State Historical Association.

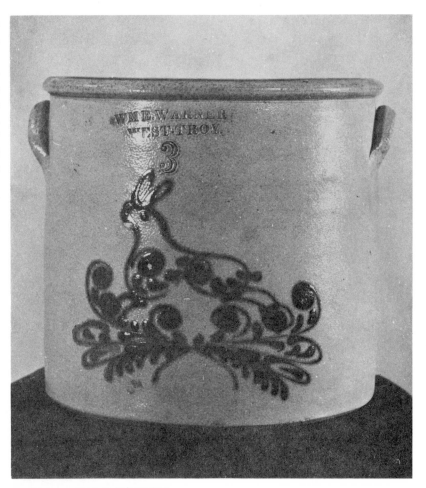

154. Unlike most surface-glazed animals, this spotted rabbit sitting up and apparently examining its paws was done with a brush rather than a slip-cup. The crock is a late New York State piece, but unmarked. As an example of how tenuous some identifications of fanciful decorations can be, what would this animal be without the obviously rabbit ears? New York State Historical Association.

127

155. As the common domestic power source, horses in a variety of actions and moods were an obvious subject for pottery decorations. This animal, on show with tail combed, neck bowed, and lifted forefoot, was incised only in bare outline and then colored with blue glaze with a brush or perhaps even the decorator's forefinger. The coloring seems to have the peculiar shading of a child's finger painting. The three-gallon jug with an unusual pouring spout was made at the Clark Pottery, and is marked in a circle "N. Clark, Jr., Athens, New York," 1843–92. Collection of Mr. & Mrs. Richard Weeks.

156. Unbridled and enjoying a run, this horse is galloping across a late New York City jug with the name of the purchaser, "Th: L. Seiter / No: 102 3th Av: [New York]" glazed in script. The decorator was certainly familiar with horses, and in rendering this scene, expressed both motion and an unfettered feeling with much greater skill than would be expected of most pottery decorators. The maker's name is not marked, but it was very possibly William Macquoid's Pottery on 12th Street in New York City. New York State Historical Association.

157. Snakes as stoneware decorations were very unusual, but when they appeared the connotation may have been as much Biblical as environmental. The serpent, extending a third of the way around this small jug, which is an unmarked Hudson Valley or New York City piece, c. 1810–30, was incised and then colored with blue glaze. Collection of Mr. John Paul Remensnyder.

158. Though the decorator no doubt meant to picture a frog in the middle of a leap, this frog almost appears to be standing and gesturing, trying to attract attention. The animal is somewhat distorted, of course, but the muscular legs and arms and the deep belly show a close familiarity with frog anatomy. The quill-traced design is toward the side rather than on the front of a two-gallon jug of the 1860's or '70's. The place of origin is unknown as the piece is unmarked. New York State Historical Association.

159. Stenciling was a most uncommon decorating technique, though there was universal experimentation with it. This spotted cow was done with blue glaze sponged over an outline cutout, probably pasted to the crock for a single use. The cutout was then removed and the spots added. The three-gallon crock was made and marked by "F. P. Goold / Brantford, [Canada West]," 1859–67. Collection of Mr. & Mrs. Andrew Brink.

160. Pigs as a source of everything from ham to lard were certainly familiar animals, and the decorator of this crock has again explored a facet of animal personality. With the direct and determined expression of someone late for a meeting, this pig is trotting along with an obvious goal in mind, and is not about to be distracted. The rapidly glazed brushstrokes add to the sense of movement. The crock is marked "W. A. Macquoid & Co. / Pottery Works / Little 12th St / New York," and dates 1863–1870. New York State Historical Association.

130

161. One of the finest early lion designs extant, the decorator who rendered this noble beast was probably influenced by scenes from early European tapestries or woodblock illustrations. The detailed incising, particularly in the lion's mane, was extremely finely done, apparently with a small multi-toothed or comb-like stylus. As a result, the lion has very much the feeling of a medieval illustration, and was brushed with a glaze so rich in cobalt-oxide that the color is more nearly black than blue. The 18th or 19th-century decorator emulating an exotic style in depicting an exotic animal, as occasionally happened, let his more familiar environment creep in. As the single incongruous note, this regal lion has what is most certainly the head and facial expression of a plain, garden-variety sheep or lamb. The crock is a New York or New Jersey piece, unmarked, *c.* 1790–1810. Collection of Mr. John Paul Remensnyder.

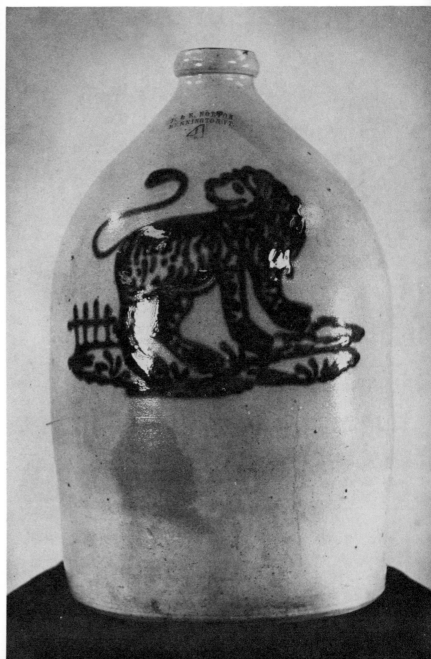

162. The Norton of Bennington lion, like the deer, was a design that became standardized by long repetition. This four-gallon jug, made *c.* 1850–59, was probably not produced as a unique item in spite of the imposing and obviously time-consuming design. The lion with his pleasant smile and swishing tail was done entirely from a slip-cup, without brushwork. Like the zebra stripes on the deer of Fort Edward fountains, the lion's leopard spots are decorator's fancy, perhaps influenced by a child's geography book with its pictures of strange wild beasts. In this scene, note the ubiquitous Norton picket fence to the left. New York State Historical Association.

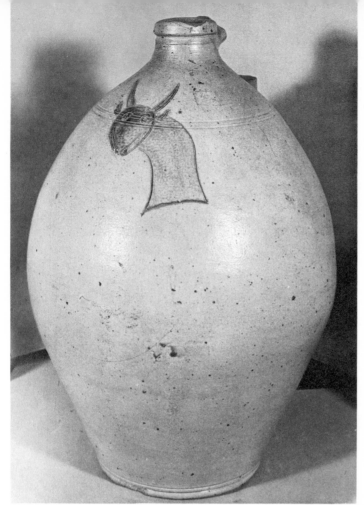

163. A goat's head—or a grinning demon —whichever it is, this strange animal head was incised in outline with ears and horns and lightly colored. It shows no great skill, but rather (at very least) a vivid imagination, and was perhaps done as a joke. The small jug by itself is a typical New York or New Jersey piece of 1820–40, and is unmarked. Collection of Mr. John Paul Remensnyder.

164. Too odd to be really described, this animal certainly bears no resemblance to anything the decorator had ever met. As closely as can be judged, the beast has the hindquarters and body of a cat which are joined to a front something similar to that of a camel or llama. Like the previous grinning head (Plate 163), the design is incised in outline and lightly colored; the jug shown here is somewhat earlier, *c.* 1820–30, and unmarked, although its shape and technique is similar to the other piece. Collection of Mr. John Paul Remensnyder.

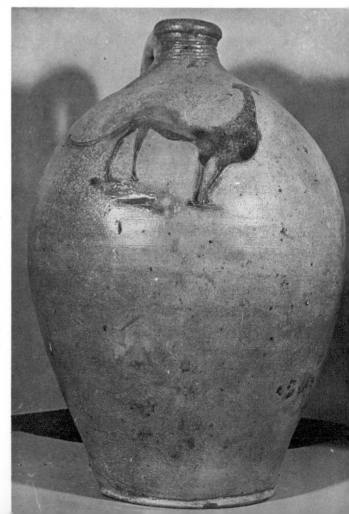

165a–b. The designs of the Albany potter Paul Cushman have been explored earlier (Plates 121–123). Nathan Clark of Athens once implied that Cushman, as well as being a poor workman, was overly fond of the bottle, and from viewing this one-gallon jar, he may have been right. The fish, birds, and ape-like but probably human figures, all incised and carelessly glazed, are at least understandable. But the long-tailed monkey with a churn and the scene of a fish milking a cow are something else again. The jar is marked with Cushman's earliest stamp and dates 1809–15. Collection of Mr. John Paul Remensnyder.

133

166. From the realm of the completely weird, the decorator's imagination or psychiatric disturbance has here taken the form of an animal-like creature with the full-face head of a cat or an owl. The head, however, is attached to the body and tail of a fish which in turn stands on bird's legs. The decorating technique is identical to that of the two designs in Plates 163–64, and the jug very similar. If we accept the distinct possibility that the three pieces could have been the work of the same hand, then we may be dealing with symptomatic rather than purely imaginative designs. Collection of Mr. John Paul Remensnyder.

167. From numbers existing today, early incised designs of fish seem to be less rare than later surface-glazed examples. Usually the reverse is true. Like all animal designs, however, fish are most uncommon in any form. Simple in technique but still striking, this rococo fish with sweeping tail is sharply incised but uncolored. Detail includes not only the scales and fins, but even tiny teeth. The unmarked jar, dating *c.* 1835–50, is unlocated but has typically New York square-ended handles. Henry Francis DuPont Winterthur Museum.

168. This simple and roughly incised fish, glazed in blue, graces a jar which is probably the unique product of Peter Peregrine Sandford of New Jersey. Sandford worked for a short time in the 1770's, and after service during the Revolution moved to White Plains, New York. This jar, which proved the existence of Sandford's pre-Revolutionary pottery, is marked "P. P. Sandford," and on the reverse side "Barbadoes Neck." Collection of Mr. John Paul Remensnyder.

169. Though not particularly elaborate, this fish with a bird's legs carrying yet another smaller fish is an extremely odd design, probably with some real significance, at least to the decorator. The serving jar with spigot bushing dates *c.* 1840 and is marked "O. V. Lewis / Greenwich," probably New York rather than Connecticut. O. V. Lewis, however, is presently unconfirmed as a pottery proprietor. Henry Ford Museum.

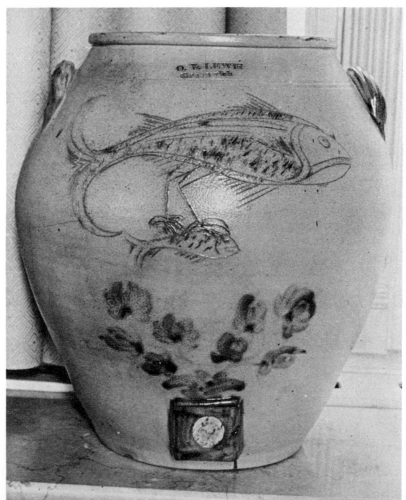

170. As another example of either an imaginary or picture-based exotic animal, no New York or New Jersey decorator ever caught a fish such as this. Though the fish is spectacular, neither the incising nor coloring are remarkable—but note how the tail has been incised over the banding previously cut on the potter's wheel. The jar itself is unidentified, dating *c.* 1830–40. Collection of Mr. John Paul Remensnyder.

171. This New York State piece is a prime example of both a small cask and a superbly incised fish. It is also quite late in date for an incised design. The well-armed sailfish or swordfish is deeply cut in the clay with good detail throughout, colored in a rich deep blue. The piece itself has the same wheel-turned banding incorporated in other Hudson River valley casks; it is inscribed, probably as a gift, "Mr. Oliver Gridley / Newburgh, July 7," and is dated 1825. Though unmarked, from other similar casks this piece could be attributed to the Clark Pottery at Athens, New York. Collection of Mr. John Paul Remensnyder.

172. As an upstate New York rendition of what is most likely a shark or an over-simplified Hudson River sturgeon, this fish, and the jar's blue glazing, show some similarity to Paul Cushman's work. The fish, however, is more neatly incised than was typical of Cushman, and the unmarked jar, *c.* 1830–50, is too late to be his. Collection of Mr. John Paul Remensnyder.

173. Almost German or Flemish in shape, this early jug marked "Boston" bears a design of what could only be a codfish. Carefully incised though it is, the fish appears almost as a large stamp. The overlaid and intersecting scales and the body lines which terminate rather than out-line across the base of fins are most unusual. The jug, though unidentified, can probably be attri-buted to Jonathan Fenton's Boston Pottery, *c.* 1794–97. Collection of Mr. John Paul Re-mensnyder.

174. This three-gallon crock, again by an upstate New York maker, has a fish incised probably quite rapidly and with no great skill, but one which somehow is more alarming than most. Perhaps the grim and determined expression and fins in disarray as if in anger make the difference. Dating c. 1840–50, again late for incised designs, the crock is marked "J. Clark & Co. / Troy [New York]." Collection of Mr. & Mrs. Richard Weeks.

175. As one of apparently few existing examples of later surface-glazed fish, this wide-eyed and incredulous creature was rapidly drawn from a slip-cup with the typical expressiveness that could be accomplished with that tool. Like most surface-glazed designs, this fish is considerably larger than earlier incised examples. The one-gallon jar, however, marked "J. M. Whitman / Havana, N.Y.," c. 1870–80, is not an elaborate piece. New York State Historical Association.

CHAPTER NINE

Scenes, Actions, and Human Figures

Probably all of the great variety of bird and animal designs on salt-glazed stoneware, in part because of their relative scarcity, appeal to us as contemporary antiquarians for many of the same reasons they were popular with the potters and decorators who made them and their original users. Like floral decorations, birds and animals represent the familiar, and while we cannot tie the precise motivations behind specific motifs to particular people, we certainly have little difficulty in appreciating or understanding the genera as a whole.

Certainly at one time or another all potters and decorators glazed bird and perhaps animal designs. There is, however, another great range of existing subjects, ranging from human faces and figures through single and even multiple scenes—many of them creations of imagination or description rather than actual observations. While such pieces are rarely encountered today, it is quite evident that occasionally stoneware decorators were motivated to go well beyond merely interpreting their familiar

environment, and into expressions of events or scenes they had only heard described, or even ideas which particularly impressed them. Though our historical hindsight can often identify superficially, it does not offer much of a clue to the personal impulses behind the most unusual designs, or to the ultimate purpose for the pieces themselves.

We have, for example, renditions of sailing ships, faces, and figures (including one based on a poem), and other similar scenes, all of which certainly took more time to depict than was required to form the pottery itself. Unlike the designs on large, special, and unique pieces such as water coolers, many of these figures and scenes, too, seem to be done on otherwise rather standard pieces of pottery—definitely not the sort that would have been extensively decorated for use as special-order items or gifts.

We are really dealing here, then, with the stoneware decorators face to face, in designs that represent the decorator's very own ideas, impulses, motivations, and expressive talents, rather than motifs mandated by proprietors or customers. The same may well be true of a few of the most unusual floral, bird, and animal decorations.

From their extreme rarity, we can assume that decorators only very infrequently indulged in designs of this nature and eloquence; certainly it was not on pottery intended for sale. Far more likely, these most imaginative of all decorations represent what the potters and decorators did for themselves, to take home for their own.

In potteries as in other producing crafts, the common assumption seems to be that in cash-scarce areas workers were sometimes paid in product. This may occasionally have been true, though there is little support for the idea in what little documentary evidence has turned up. There is no doubt, however, that pottery workers were commonly permitted to make pottery for themselves, in fact many small and unique pieces, in particular, were probably never made in quantity for sale, but simply for the potters themselves.

In the not necessarily odd but certainly unique and unexpected renderings on these pieces, then, we have the individually unique work of numbers of different decorators doing designs for their own enjoyment —often tongue-in-cheek and showing great humor, sometimes with a firm image in mind, or perhaps experimentally, just to see what the end result will be. All of these decorators, though, had a common and basic feeling for and rapport with the clay— there is no sense of groping or hesitancy. When we look at these individualistic and personal expressions, more than with any other decorative subject we have reason to regret the anonymity of the decorators. They never signed even personal pieces, much less their routine work, so that all but their most striking results are lost to us forever.

176a–b–c. A three-gallon jug with three incised scenes, this piece is unmarked, but certainly came from a Germanic language area of southeastern Pennsylvania. The first scene (176a, left) is of a curiously New England saltbox house, what could pass for a palm tree (but probably is not), and a small outbuilding labled in script "Smoke / haus." Next comes a sloop (176b, below) with square topsail evidently carrying a cargo of unidentifiable animals, the hull incised, and also in script the word "Gleassor.'' Finally, the sloop nears an island (176c, lower left) and strange conglomeration of buildings labeled "Head Haus," "Enclo.," and "Sluss[?] haus." The second story doorway is aptly marked "Dore." The crude incising is also crudely glazed. The scenes and action are inexplicable now. The jug dates c. 1820–50. Henry Francis DuPont Winterthur Museum.

177. The War of 1812 was the obvious inspiration behind a number of naval scenes. This presentation jug, *c.* 1818–20, is another war-stimulated piece, and was made for a Captain Stewart of Hartford by Daniel Goodale. The incised lines of the frigate under sail have been blue glazed; the jug is marked "D. Goodale / Hartford" and "Stewart / Hartford." Goodale made numbers of other known presentation pieces, most with extensive incised decorations. Henry Ford Museum.

178. With its incised design of a sailing vessel complete even to hatted sailors on deck, this jug was done by an unidentified New England potter, probably during or immediately following the war. The incised lines have been dry glazed; the sails, hull, and waves are completely colored. Old Sturbridge Village.

179 a–b–c. Crude as the incising may be, the three expressive ships make this jar one of the finest early incised pieces known today, and very likely a piece motivated by news of a victorious sea battle. Each of the three vessels sailing around the jar is, from its banners and punch-incised gunports, an American warship, and each is towing a dismasted prize. The two bands of distinctive coggle banding around the neck make it possible to attribute the piece to the Warne & Letts Pottery of Cheesequake, New Jersey, where shards showing identical coggling have been excavated. From the scene, the date of the jar may well be 1812 or 1813, when the U.S., to its own amazement and joy, was victorious in several single-ship battles with the British. The jar had been previously recorded, certainly erroneously, as a product of James Morgan. Philadelphia Museum of Art.

143

180. Decorations depicting real action are extremely rare; and like incised sailing vessels, probably only a very few examples exist. This incised scene of a man in tights doing a backflip from a galloping horse could only have been motivated by a trip to the circus. The jar appears to be a New England piece of about 1840. The only marking is "James Alexander" in script below the combed band, either the man for whom the jar was made or, just possibly, the signature of the decorator. Henry Ford Museum.

181. Except on very special pieces, themselves rare, full scenes or expressions of action are unusual. This five-gallon crock, in form an ordinary production piece, bears a surface-glazed design, done with both brush and slip-cup of a tree that extends over the full side. A marsh extends around the base, and to the left of the tree two ducks are taking off from it. The crock is marked "Fort Edward Pottery Co. / Fort Edward, N.Y." Collection of Mr. & Mrs. Richard Weeks.

182. Of all the varied designs found on stoneware, those of human faces or figures are often the most striking. The designs on pottery by William Macquoid & Co. of New York City are always interesting and lively. This glaze-painted cherub with angel wings and a pendant cross is no exception, and it graces a one-and-a-half-gallon jar of the 1860's. New York Historical Society.

183. Another example of similarity of style in distinctive design, this two-gallon jar is a piece made and marked on order for a Glens Falls, New York merchant who obviously did not make the piece himself. The surface-glazed design is a full farm scene complete with post and rail fences and a tall spruce tree on the left. The style is, in fact, identical to that of the standard Norton of Bennington decorations and can certainly be attributed to either Bennington, or possibly the Fort Edward Pottery Company, Fort Edward, New York —both within easy marketing range of Glen Falls! New York State Historical Association.

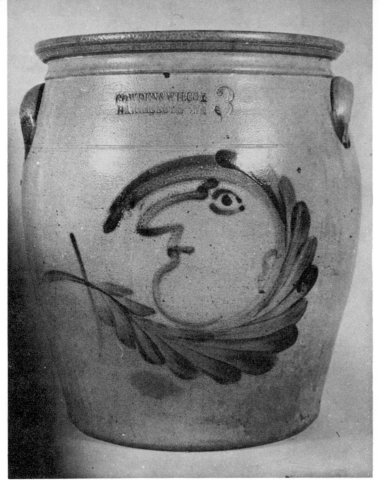

184. The face of a round-chined Punch, brush glazed and enclosed within a wreath, was one of a number of odd designs used by Cowden & Wilcox (another was a cow jumping over the moon), a firm known for its many rather elaborate decorations on otherwise standard pieces of pottery. This three-gallon crock, dated *c.* 1850–60, is marked "Cowden & Wilcox / Harrisburg, Pa." Collection of the author.

185.   I shot an arrow into the air,
      It fell to earth, I knew not where. . . .
      I breathed a song into the air;
      It fell to earth, I knew not where. . . .
      Long long afterward in an oak
      I found the arrow still unbroke;
      And the song, from beginning to end,
      I found again in the heart of a friend.

Only the lines of Longfellow's "The Arrow and the Song" can possibly explain this well-dressed young man half-way up a white oak—obviously retrieving his arrow. The wings or heart behind him very likely refer to the song. The jar, by an unknown maker, is not only incised, but once the clay had partially dried, the major lines—the tree trunk, face, and heart—were sculptured crudely with a knife. Finally, the lines were blue glazed. Collection of Mr. John Paul Remensnyder.

186. Another piece from the age of the romantic poets, this tall jar with its atypical applied handles is an upstate New York piece, but unmarked and by an unidentified maker. The scene is of a long-gowned woman in dress of the 1830's or '40's in a grove of tall Lombardy poplars—all very skillfully applied in brushed glaze which achieves both good shading and an impression of detail which is not really there. New York State Historical Association.

187. A jug to end all jugs, the decorator of this piece has given us a picture of three girls at the beach, perhaps Atlantic City. The standing girl poses coyly; the bathing suits were either the bikinis of the 1890's or, just possibly, the girls' underwear. The figures, blue glazed with slip-cup and brush, are certainly a far cry from any usual decoration—perhaps the decorator was adding to his own collection. The three-gallon jug is stamped "Fulper Bros. / Flemington, N. J." New York State Historical Association.

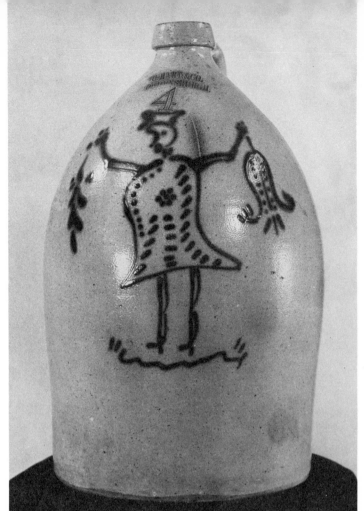

188. A strange design, this figure in blue glaze is holding in one hand what could be either a fish or an ear of corn; from the other hand he pours some sort of liquid. The four-gallon jug was produced by Charles Hart, Jr., during 1850–1858 at his pottery in Ogdensburgh, New York. New York State Historical Association.

189. A few, but a very few, decorators produced an occasional cartoon, such as this line scene of a quite surprised man meeting a strange figure. Who can tell today the object of the piece? The covered jar, *c.* 1860–70, was made by "Cowden & Wilcox" of Harrisburg, Pa. New York State Historical Association.

CHAPTER TEN

Relief Designs, Pressing, and Molding

Incising and glazing was not the limit of decoration on American stoneware, for stoneware itself was a flexible medium in which potters could and did engage in flights of ornamental fancy. Though basic vessels may have been turned on wheels and hand produced before the mid-19th century, applied parts—handles, spouts, and spigot bushings—were formed in molds or from patterns. It was hardly difficult to utilize the same technique to create three-dimensional details.

Molded decorations are often found on early European stoneware—the faces on German Bartmannkrüge jugs and the decorative flourishes on English Fulham pottery. As with incising and glazing, there certainly existed a strong European tradition of molded ornamentation, both in the potters' own background, and in European pottery brought to America. Again, though, it would appear that practical necessity and productive efficiency outweighed tradition, for there are relatively few existing American pieces with molded decorations and most seem again to have been specially made.

Molding and applied decoration generally sprang from the same environmental motivations as incising and glazing. Patriotic motifs predominated—particularily busts of George Washington, and eagles—designs that could logically be formed in or pressed from small molds. Flower and leaf designs, on the other hand, were uncommon, probably because they required the forming of thin stems and flat sections difficult to mold or apply. The most elaborate examples of stoneware with applied moldings seem almost to be exercises in rococo construction and ultimate detail—pieces with vast profusions of small knobs and escutcheons, wound ropes, and strange patterns. The rococo examples alone must have been extremely time-consuming exercises, and for this reason they are extremely rare. In any event, molded decorations, particularly applied ones, were tricky things to form, and like elaborate incising, were not compatible with quantity production until they could be accomplished as a unified operation in the molding of entire pieces of pottery.

This decorative three-dimensional molding could be accomplished in one of two ways—by pressing a stamp into the body of a freshly turned and wet pot so that the result was a raised figure, or by applying a separately fashioned piece from a mold. The latter was the usual system, and it is not difficult to spot the difference. Designs formed simply by pressing a mold to the wet surface of a pot would result in a figure that, while it appeared in relief, was quite shallow and usually did not stand out beyond the surface of the vessel. Applied decorations, conversely, stand out very sharply in relief, obviously as additional pieces of clay, and will very often show a seam or apparent corner where they have been applied to the body of the pot itself. The third and much more common form was a simple stamp in which the design was pressed into the body of the pot and below its surface. (See chapter eleven for detailed discussion.)

The molds for applied decorations were usually of clay which had been formed around an original pattern and then fired, or wood which was carved out to form a decoration. The potter would first wet the mold so that the final piece cou d be released. Then the wet clay was pressed into it tightly. The back surface of the clay design the potter would then scrape off with a knife, flush with the mold. Finally, the design could either be peeled out and applied to the side of a pot by hand, or the mold containing the clay decoration could be pressed and then withdrawn, leaving the design applied. Once separate decorations had been applied, the pot could then be incised (if this was intended) and then dried, glazed, and fired as a unit, with the decoration firmly in place.

Later in the 19th century, after the introduction of mass-production molding techniques and machinery, molded decorations became quite common. These, however, were formed as single units with the molded pottery itself, usually by casting near-fluid clay in a two- or four-piece mold. At this stage, though, even the pottery was no longer an artistic product, and these later molded decorations cannot really be considered in the same light as the earlier hand-applied types.

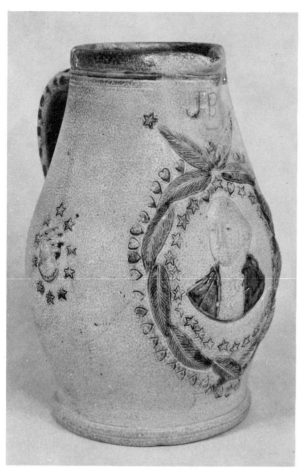

190. As an example of a rather flat relief molding, this bust of George Washington was formed by pressing a stamp to the body of the pitcher without additional applied clay. The pitcher is an elaborate one, however, with its circles around the bust, first of stamped stars, then an incised wreath of intertwined leaves, and finally a circle of stamped hearts. Note the small applied head in relief, surrounded by stamped stars, on the side of the pitcher. The marking "J. B." in incised letters is unidentified, but the pitcher most probably is from New Jersey or Pennsylvania. Henry Francis DuPont Winterthur Museum.

191. The reverse side of the wonderfully incised "T. Whiteman" piece (Plate 148), this cooler or fountain bears a medallion in relief of the American eagle so well done that the technique is hard to determine. Since the eagle and stars are raised from a slight depression, the design was probably pressed directly, and not applied as an additional piece of clay. The extremely sharp and detailed incised tree is duplicated, with a bird and large fish, on the other side; the date, 1853, is incised here. Henry Francis DuPont Winterthur Museum.

192. On a New York State jug of 1820–40, this bust of George Washington is clearly a separately applied molding, for though no seam is readily apparent, the design stands out sharply in relief and is raised well above the surface. Stamps were used to make the impressed rosettes and the legend "G. Washington / For. Ever." Henry Francis DuPont Winterthur Museum.

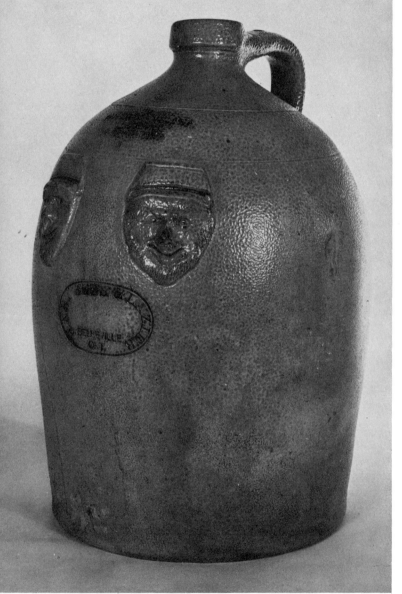

193. In a very similar manner to the preceding piece (Plate 192), this much later jug, probably of the 1880's, has been decorated with shallow, applied toby masks with military uniform caps. The mold may have been washed with blue glaze before each mask was formed. As well as a distiller's mark, the jug was stamped "Hart Bros. & Lazier / Belleville, Ont.," 1879–1914. National Museum of Canada.

152

194. To say nothing of the multiple applied moldings, this flowerpot is a most unusual piece in that it is coated with white clay slip, and not saltglazed. The rather crude and obviously separate moldings are then blueglazed. The flower pot is American, but of unknown origin, and dates from the mid-19th century. Henry Francis DuPont Winterthur Museum.

195. This very detailed eagle in relief shows clearly the seam and corner of a separately applied molding. The eagle was first formed in a mold, then applied to the pitcher very much like a modern decal transfer. The rest of the design was then incised, dried, and glazed. Though unmarked, the incised leaf decoration is quite characteristic of the work of the Remmeys; this pitcher is attributed to Richard C. Remmey of Philadelphia. Philadelphia Museum of Art.

153

196. An extreme example of applied decoration, this water cooler has attached to it coils of clay around the handle loops, tiny dots in relief, and around the upper spout, a collar of pieces cut as tapered strips and laid on the main body of the jug. Note that the small discs applied to the handles and the upper parts of the collar strips have been impressed to appear as screw heads. Added to all of this is some incising, a fringe of stamped circles below the collar strips, and even tulips brushed in blue glaze. Virtually every technique of stoneware decoration is included in this single piece. Philadelphia Museum of Art.

197. A good example of an elaborate separately applied molded decoration, this American eagle flanked by cornucopias graces an otherwise ordinary eight-gallon jar. The floral decoration in blue slip is of little importance. The jar, probably a New York or New Jersey piece of c. 1850–60, is unmarked. Henry Ford Museum.

154

198. With the marks of hand shaping accentuated and remaining, this jug of a most unusual shape was presented, as marked, by "E. Hall, Ohio to John Coll / ings." The clasped hands of peace were probably applied as unmolded strips of clay and then sculptured. The flower is of separately applied pieces formed by hand. The jug is covered with small die-cut discs—the two in the centers of the coiled rope have been stamped to resemble screw heads, as have those below the finely formed handle. E. Hall is the attributed maker; the piece is dated about 1858. Brooklyn Museum.

199. In a decorative style typical of red earthenware potters, this large serving jar has very extensive and excellent molded oak leaves and acorns applied to either side, with molded branches forming the handles. The blue-glazed bird, perhaps an eagle, seems here an incongruous addition. The initials "F. L. T.," framed in interlocking loops of applied clay, may refer to either an individual or an organization. The large jar is marked above the base "Johnson & Baldwin," of Akron, Ohio, c. 1860. Henry Ford Museum.

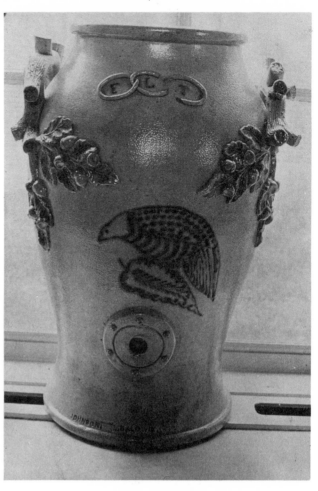

200. With knobs, this studded cooler seems to be a piece begun without a plan and allowed to grow topsy-turvy. The knob of the cover is the modeled figure of a child. The cooler itself was heavily coggled with crossing lines and squares. Then each of the small knobs was attached as a pointed finger-formed blob of clay, and finally the point of each was impressed with a stamp to give the knob the appearance of a barnacle. All manner of significance can be read into a piece such as this, but if nothing else, the potter was imaginative. Metropolitan Museum of Art.

CHAPTER ELEVEN

Stamps

The decorative process was always a great problem in potteries engaged in the business of producing identical or similar forms in great quantity. On the one hand, aesthetics and competitive situations demanded decoration, but time, materials, and the final breakage rate in firing conspired to make elaborate decoration uneconomical. Decorators, too, could never really keep pace with the primary production of the potters, which was, of course, the reason that so much stoneware at many potteries bore little if any decoration. Potters had always been concerned with a need to speed up the decorative process in hopes of producing a greater proportion of decorated pieces. Thus purely mechanical decoration, done with small stamps and dies which could be quickly pressed into wet clay, was universal in Europe before stoneware was ever thought of in North America. The early Saxons decorated pottery with stamps cut particularily for that purpose; German stoneware bore stamped designs from about 1400 on, and English Nottingham stoneware of the 18th century combined incising, coggle banding, and stamping with unexcelled detail and delicacy.

With the attributes of requiring little artistic skill and less time, the range in variation of stamped impressions was almost endless, depending only on the number of stamps a potter could make up or accumulate. Single stamps could press a complete design, or could be used to do the most difficult parts of a hand-incised decoration, such as the center of a flower. In fact, many decorations were combinations of incising and stamping, for the result and appearance (indentations in the clay) was the same. In other fashions, the multiple use of several stamps could create quite intricate patterns on the surface of a pot with no real handwork whatsoever. Essentially, the decorator with hand stamps could produce in a few seconds what would take minutes to incise by hand.

The tools for different forms of stamping and pressing could really be anything that would leave an impression; used most often were small dies. The dies themselves were often made of clay, originally formed from a pattern and then fired. Since impressing in clay was much the same as printing on paper, many stamps were surface-carved wooden blocks. A great number of ready-made designs could be pressed directly from the printers' cast-lead decorative vignettes, which after about 1800 were available from type founders. Line designs—borders, circles, hearts, diamonds, and the like—were often stamped from small dies, wooden blocks, or handles with the design set in as a metal rim. The same dies cou d be used for cutting small devices from rolled clay sheets for applied designs.

Another form of stamping, which had to be done before the freshly turned pot was removed from the wheel, was banding or coggling. The coggle wheel was nothing but a forked handle which was mounted on a small wheel with a decoration cut in its circumference. A coggled band was pressed by slowly rotating the pottery on the potter's wheel, and letting the coggle wheel turn carefully against it.

Coggles most usually were wooden wheels. Sometimes, though not always, they were specially carved. A grooved wheel, for example, would impress a band of two or more lines; a clock gear would produce a line of crimp marks. Like plain stamps, coggle wheels could be reproduced in pottery by first making a mold from the original.

Hand stamps, metal-edged dies, and coggle wheels often bore designs unique to particular potteries. Thus given one or more known pieces, identical impressions and coggled decorations, like characteristic incised or glazed designs, are very often strong evidence for attributing unmarked pottery to specific makers.

At least a proportion of early stoneware was marked by the maker; after 1840 virtually all was marked, either with the name of the pottery or that of the merchant for whom an order was made. Earlier printed markings, such as the "Liberty Forev./ Warne & Letts / S. Amboy, N. Jersey" or the "Paul Cushman's Stoneware Factory 1800 / Half a Mile West of the Albany Gaol" stampings, were pressed from single hand-cut wooden blocks. These may also have been duplicated in pottery. All of the later markings, however, were in one way or another made from lead printers' type. Loose type could easily be fixed in a grooved block, and would stamp pottery as readily as it would print ink. With a font or two of type in his shop, a potter had no difficulty putting together a stamp to mark jugs or crocks with whatever specific label a particular customer might want. Capacity markings, too, usually on gallon vessels, were pressed from single large pieces of type.

Once the pottery was dried, stamped, and impressed, markings could be glazed with powdered or liquid cobalt glaze exactly as any incised design. The result from the simplest possible processes was completely satisfactory.

201. A pitcher of a rather European shape, this early piece is inscribed "Capt. Adam Baily." Below the name is a row of pressed or stamped swags and pendants. From the spacing, each impression was made separately with a hand stamp; the design was not laid with a coggle wheel. The decoration was then brushed with blue glaze. The pitcher is unmarked and cannot be precisely located, but the design is very similar to that impressed in other pieces made in the Boston, Massachusetts area, *c.* 1800–1810. Collection of Mr. John Paul Remensnyder.

202. This jug of an unusually classic and pure shape is decorated with only three truncated semicircles and spaced blossoms. Each segment of the design was a separate impression. The stamps for the semicircles may have incorporated the five small circles within each, though spacing again would indicate that these were again separately pressed. The jug is unmarked, but is probably of Boston origin, and dated *c.* 1790–1810. Collection of Mr. John Paul Remensnyder.

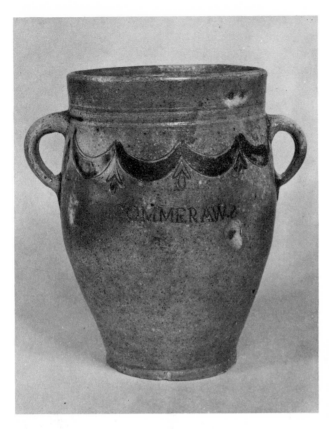

203. A very handsome one-gallon crock, this piece is decorated with a row of swags and pendants similar in outline, if not in detail, to that on the earlier Boston piece (Plate 201). Again each swag and each pendant was a separate impression with a hand stamp. Impressed swag and pendant, and swag and tassel designs, though with great regional variation, were a common and widely used motif on stoneware of the late 18th and early 19th centuries. The "Commeraws" marking is that of Thomas Commeraw, a New York City potter of the late 18th and early 19th centuries. Henry Francis DuPont Winterthur Museum.

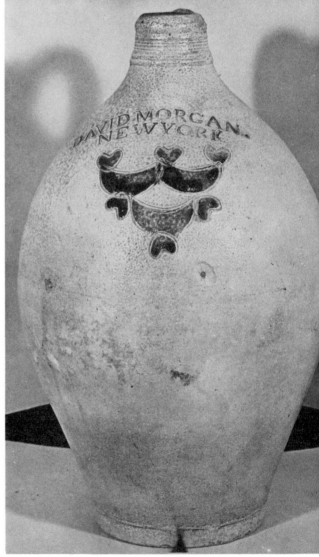

204. An early 19th-century New York City piece, this little half-gallon jug is decorated with separately impressed and colored half-moons and hearts. The design complex was pressed somewhat carelessly; impressions overlap in several places. The jug is marked "David Morgan / New York." Collection of Mr. John Paul Remensnyder.

205. With a design of rather unusual scalloped-edged swags and hanging tassels, this very simple two-gallon crock is probably from New Jersey, c. 1800–1810. Like virtually all such designs, the swags and tassels are separately pressed and later colored with blue glaze. The jar is unmarked; while the swags are similar in shape to the design on the following piece (Plate 206), they are probably not sufficiently similar to warrant an attribution. Collection of Mr. John Paul Remensnyder.

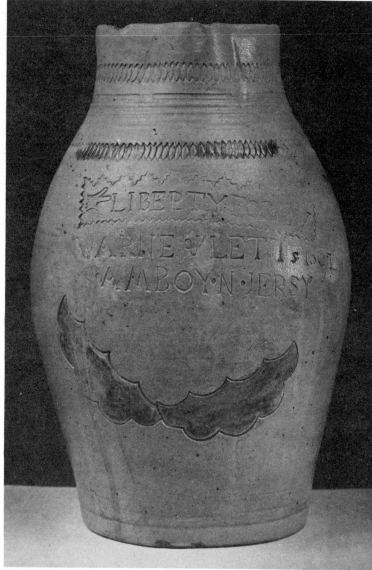

206. With a complete range of impressed design on one piece, this large serving pitcher was first inscribed with bands on the potter's wheel, and then given two decorative diamond-patterned bands impressed from a coggle wheel. Below the coggled band is a stamp impressed from a single block, "Liberty Forev.," within a decorative border. Below this legend the piece is marked, again with a large stamp, "Warne & Letts. 1807 / S. Amboy, N. Jersy." Finally below the lettering is an impressed design of two scalloped-edged half-moons somewhat similar to the swags on the previous piece (Plate 205), though of far larger size. The pottery and partnership of Thomas Warne and Joshua Letts operated at South Amboy, New Jersey from 1805 to 1813. Brooklyn Museum.

207. With the typical New Jersey double row of coggled banding setting off wheel-cut bands, the coggle wheel which applied the bands on this piece probably looked like a toothed gear, in fact, it may well have been a discarded clock gear. The jar, dated *c.* 1790–1810, was decorated as well with a three-petaled or bladed impressed motif and blue surface glaze. The letters above the decorations, "X. P.," probably hand incised, are the initials of Xerxes Price, who operated a pottery at Roundabout, New Jersey. Brooklyn Museum.

208. Coggled banding, as a primary decoration with blue glaze added, was often used on small pieces. The coggle wheel for this banding was not a wide roller that impressed the entire design at once, but rather it pressed a single zigzag. Note that in the lower band a second turning of the crock under the coggle wheel has overlaid the design. So, too, the upper zigzag band, while itself not overlapped, seems to cover a previously incised band. By an unidentified New York City or New Jersey maker, the jar dates *c.* 1815–30. Collection of Mr. John Paul Remensnyder.

209. Coggled banding, since coggle wheels were unique to particular potteries, and yet pressed a standardized design, can be extremely useful as evidence for making attributions. This small crock, standing only about five inches high, is unmarked and decorated solely by two coggled bands flanking wheel-turned bands—alone rather indicative of New Jersey origin. The pattern of the coggling, however, is identical to that on the handsome three-warship crock (Plate 179 a–b–c), even to the small German pinwheel flower within every other large lozenge. The design in this case identifies the maker of both pieces, for shards with identical coggling have been recovered from the site of the Warne & Letts pottery at Cheesequake, New Jersey. Collection of Mr. John Paul Remensnyder.

210. A plain marking, impressed with no real decorative intent, is very often the only adornment a piece of stoneware has. This marking, "Boston. / 1804," on a three-gallon jar, has never been precisely identified. From the handles, the jar dates *c.* 1804–20. The marking is commonly found both alone and in combination with impressed swags and tassels; the date probably refers to the date of establishment of the unidentified Boston pottery which produced the piece. Old Sturbridge Village.

211. This early jar, with its cover missing, bears only the single decorative mark "Boston," enclosed within a banner resembling a sea serpent and impressed from a single stamp. The pottery which used this device has not been established, but it could be a mark of Jonathan Fenton, 1794–97. Collection of Mr. John Paul Remensnyder.

212. Paul Cushman of Albany, as might be expected, used a longer and more elaborate name stamp on his earliest work than any other known maker. This tall jar, with no other decoration or blue glaze, is marked simply "Paul Cushman's Stoneware Factory, 1809 / Half a Mile West of the Albany Gaol." The stamp is probably his first, used from 1809 to 1811. Albany Institute of History & Art.

213a–b. This covered jar, coated with a brown Albany slip, is marked simply "Paul Cushman." Cushman, however, then applied over the brown Albany slip a blue glaze around the handle terminals and over the name stamp. This jar, however, has a very unusual wooden cover (below) marked in raised letters, around which the wood was shaved away, "Amey* Kent*of Rome*/preserv'd*Gra. Pes/1810*." Henry Francis DuPont Winterthur Museum.

214. One use of the stamped marking was to indicate contents. This three-gallon serving jug with applied double-looped handles and a bushing for a spigot below, is stamped twice "Cognac-Brandy / 1820," all within a border of blue surface glaze. The jug is not so marked, but is known to have been made by the Nathan Clark Pottery at Athens, New York. Here the date 1820 seems to indicate the actual year of manufacture. New York State Historical Association.

215a–b. The Charlestown Massachusetts Pottery, in combination with a name stamp, often used small impressed decorative devices, very often in groups of three. This jug, for example, has below the name "Charlestown" three tiny impressed eagles, each applied separately with a hand stamp. Old Sturbridge Village.

216. Another Charlestown jug, somewhat later than the previous piece (Plates 215a–b), has above the name a single decorative stamp of an eagle perched atop a cannon. Typically, the Charlestown marking and decorative stamps were not blue glazed. The Charlestown stamp was the earliest mark of Barnabus Edmands and William Burroughs, who established a pottery in 1821. Collection of Mr. John Paul Remensnyder.

217. As on previous pieces (Plates 44, 45, & 46) floral stamps were sometimes used alone. This jar is decorated with four rosettes which are fairly complex in structure. The hand stamp itself was probably formed of clay rather than metal or wood. Such a rosette, though standing alone here, could easily have been used to form the center of a much larger incised flower. The unmarked jar dates c. 1790–1810, and was probably a product of Clarkson Crolius of New York. Collection of Mr. John Paul Remensnyder.

218. The stamp on this jar, of a face in profile within a rosette, was impressed from a single die. The jar itself, with an inset for the handles and a heavy top, is extremely unusual. The stamp was a mark of the Old Bridge, New Jersey Pottery, established in 1805 by James Morgan Jr. & Jacob and Nicholas van Winkle. It operated until *c.* 1840. Collection of Mr. John Paul Remensnyder.

219. Impressed decorative motifs, like coggled banding, were most typically used on stoneware of the early 19th century, during the period of incised decorations. Except for pottery names and capacity figures, stampings nearly disappeared in the later period of surface-glazed decorations. This impressed swan, however, about two inches long and with lines colored in blue, graces a New York State two-gallon jug of the 1880's or perhaps '90's. Such late stamps are extremely unusual. The jug itself is unmarked, and except for the impressed swan is undistinguished. Collection of the author.

CHAPTER TWELVE

Miscellaneous Functional Pieces

The use of stoneware as a creative medium never reached the heights of craftsmanship or delicacy in North America that it did in England or Germany. In spite of solid crocks, jars, and jugs being by far the most common product of most potteries, however, American stoneware was not limited to these forms alone. In fact, a vast variety of small objects, most of which were primarily utilitarian rather than decorative, were made from time to time at virtually all potteries, though with few exceptions apparently not often in as great number as the heavier pieces.

Of all these varied small forms, pitchers, flowerpots, and bottles alone were standard stock items, usually shown on potters' price lists (Plates 293–300). Stoneware bottles in particular, as trade rather than consumer items, with wide design variation, were made in large quantity virtually everywhere, and these are covered in chapter thirteen.

Small stoneware utensils, however, whether made as unique pieces or in lots of dozens or hundreds, are appealing mainly because of their forms and designs and, of course, relative rarity. Most have little if any real decoration and, like bottles, skillfully or elaborately ornamented pieces are scarce indeed.

If we were to place stoneware, in a socio-economic reference, between woodenware and pewter, the assumption is unavoidable that some small utensils—such things as mugs, porringers, inkwells, pitchers, and jars—must at one time have been in extremely common and widespread use. This assumption is often supported by evidence of actual production, the quantity of fragments and shards of such pieces that are unearthed whenever early pottery sites are excavated. Contemporary rough usage we can take for granted, but even allowing for this, the paucity of these items today indicates an uncommonly low survival rate.

Many of the small utilitarian pieces show specially careful rather than routine craftsmanship, for these were the pieces often made as unique products on individual order, as gifts to relatives or special customers and probably also as apprentice exercises. Crocks and jugs were turned on wheels; the smaller pieces often required mastering techniques of molding and applying thin flat sections as well, in such a way that the end results would not crack in firing.

Conversely, other small pieces are among the very simplest and most totally unornamented of all stoneware forms. Good examples are the ale mug, Plate 233, the crude porringer, Plate 236, or the inkwell, Plate 245. In their own era such items as these were obviously the most basic of household pottery, with no aesthetic implication or function whatsoever. Today, of course, they are to us reflections of the culture of their age, and rare as well. Hence they have become extremely desirable.

As is also true of bottles, small functional objects are often examples of the best work of stoneware potters, and appear in an unending variety of individualized shapes and forms, to say nothing of functions. Few were marked by their makers, and many, without attributable characteristics and removed from their original areas, cannot even be placed in a particular location.

Even the most elaborate of the smaller pieces, however, such as "The Blind Pig" cooler (Plate 242), were not forms on which decorators lavished their skills and imagination. Rather, the separate decoration of the small pieces is usually superficial; the decorators preferred to do their more elaborate work on the largest pieces. Thus, like bottles, these extremely varied utilitarian objects are folk art in clay rather than of incising or glazing, a credit to the potters who made them.

220. Small pitchers, even without decoration, usually can be assumed to be specially made pieces. Most stoneware makers' price lists include pitchers of one quart or larger, but rarely smaller cream or sauce pitchers. This extremely rare piece, embellished with a rather crudely incised, glazed bird and vine, holds something less than a quart and stands about eight inches high. Its shape is much like that of most larger pitchers of the mid-19th century, and it is marked below the handle "M. S. / August the 9, 1873." It may be a product of the Remmey family of Philadelphia. Collection of Mr. John Paul Remensnyder.

221. This small pitcher from the late 19th century in its coggled bands shows the influence of the contemporary German pottery which was beginning to come on to the market at this time. Note that the small bands of dots overlap, indicating that each was done separately from the wide center bands. In addition to the coggling, simple blue-glazed floral designs have been added to the body of the pitcher. This piece was made by R. C. Remmey, a descendant of the Remmey family of New York City. Philadelphia Museum of Art. Photograph by A. J. Wyatt.

222. Standing only about five inches high and holding less than a pint, this cream pitcher was decorated with a few simple brushstrokes of blue glaze. The molded handle indicates that it was a piece made in at least sufficient quantity to justify the mold. The salt-glazed inside is most unusual, for the insides of virtually all 19th-century stoneware vessels were coated with brown Albany slip. Collection of Mr. John Paul Remensnyder.

223. Either a pitcher without a pouring lip or a jar missing its cover, this small piece is quite possibly European rather than American, though in the absence of a maker's mark it is impossible to be sure. The evidently pulled handle (i.e., pulled and formed at the top directly from the body of the piece as it was being shaped, rather than separately made and applied) is extremely unusual on American stoneware. The beading and banding at the top and base has the appearance of having been formed with a coggle wheel; the leaf designs were incised, and the blue glaze then added. Altogether, it is a mysterious piece. Collection of Mr. John Paul Remensnyder.

172

224. True miniature pieces standing no more than two or three inches high are very unusual, but most miniatures are also quite late. These miniature pitchers and cruets, all with very simple design and decoration, date probably from the 1880's or '90's, and were made in Pennsylvania. While some miniature pieces were made as toys, others were made either as samples or for particular household purposes. Henry Francis DuPont Winterthur Museum.

225. With its incised decorations and earlike handles, this covered jar would appear to be quite early, but in fact it probably dates from the late 19th or possibly early 20th century. The design of blue-glazed, incised hearts with unglazed intersecting hearts within suggests possible Pennsylvania origin. The pottery is not discolored, indicating careful temperature control in firing, but the designs are neither as carefully done nor as crisp and sharp as the incised designs found on earlier pieces. Henry DuPont Winterthur Museum.

226. Made by the famous John Bell Pottery of Waynesboro, Pennsylvania, this canning jar, though lacking its cover, is recessed on top for a sealing ring and grooved around its neck for a wire loop. The very faded house in blue glaze decorating one side of the jar is most unusual; the opposite side is decorated with a small bird. The jar dates from the 1870's or early 80's, and is made of the Bell Pottery's typical grayish-green stoneware. Collection of Mrs. Tracy Cone.

227. This jar has perhaps one of the most unusual tops ever fashioned—a terraced cone fully as tall as the jar itself. The blue-glazed floral decoration in this case is unimportant; it is the design of the jar itself which makes the piece intriguing. Though probably from the mid-19th century, the origin of this piece is unknown. Henry Francis DuPont Winterthur Museum.

228. In addition to the unusual domed top, this covered jar has handles of simple rolled pieces of clay which appear almost as coiled animals or serpents' heads. The jar is too small to have many logical uses, and it is unmarked. The grayish-green color of the clay, however, and the rather greenish-blue glazed decoration, is very suggestive of the John Bell Pottery of Waynesboro, Pennsylvania. Henry Francis DuPont Winterthur Museum.

229. A simple undecorated canning jar of the late 19th century, this piece once had an angular-sided cover which was probably sealed with wax. Like most such simple pieces, this jar is unmarked, but came from Cortland, New York, and can possibly be attributed to the Madison Woodruff Pottery. Collection of the author.

230. Either a jar or more likely a flower vase, this piece is possibly of European origin. The strange double-line incised border is quite unusual, and on both sides of the piece a stalk with simple leaves extends from the base to the border. The small grid pattern to the right was applied with a stamp, again without logical explanation. The border and entire rim are coated with heavy blue glaze. Henry Francis DuPont Winterthur Museum.

231. This miniature teapot, with a finely incised decoration on each side, dates from the early 19th century and is probably of New Jersey or Pennsylvania origin. This piece is extremely unusual in that it is not salt glazed, but rather has been covered with a white slip over the bare pottery; the white slip then was covered by the cobalt blue decorative glaze. This form of glazing is only rarely seen on stoneware pottery, and was accomplished by double firing; i.e., the piece was first fired with the white slip coating, and then decorated in blue and refired. Henry Francis DuPont Winterthur Museum.

232. Some household utensils were more readily fashioned from stoneware than others; among the least common of stoneware pieces are eating utensils. This stoneware egg cup, probably from Pennsylvania, dates from the early 19th century. The horizontal stem and the leaves around the cup were not really incised, but were lightly scratched in the clay before coloring. The scalloping around the top edge is entirely brushwork. Henry Francis DuPont Winterthur Museum.

233. Every inn was once well equipped with just such crude and common utensils as this plain 18th-century ale mug. Unmarked and unadorned, it is a purely utilitarian piece, but one which, even to its warped and wavy lip, has a great romantic appeal and seems to call for a stone fireplace, dark beams, and flickering lamps. Collection of Mr. John Paul Remensnyder.

234. One of the smallest and earliest known dated pieces of American stoneware, this beer or ale mug is quite heavily formed. From the even and symmetrical banding and grooving, it is obviously the work of a skilled potter. The design and date 1773 are in blue surface glaze. The piece is unmarked, and superficially might seem to be later than the glazed date. The date, however, conforms to the active period of the probable maker. The design of a double scroll and dots scattered in a diamond pattern, here visible on the right side, is very characteristic of the work and other known pieces of Abraham Mead of Greenwich, Connecticut. He was active as an apprentice and independent potter *c.* 1755–90; this mug can probably be attributed to him. Collection of Mr. John Paul Remensnyder.

235. Such pieces as coffee cups are far more unusual than mugs. The cup on the left is very imaginatively decorated around the outside with incised free flowing lines. The inside is washed with brown Albany slip which has mottled in firing. The mug on the right is rather crudely made and probably a volume-production piece. Both date from the mid-19th century but are of unknown origins. Henry Francis DuPont Winterthur Museum.

236. A once universal but long defunct form of general eating cup was the porringer, a sort of combination coffee cup and soup bowl. Used for everything from soup to stews, most household porringers were of red earthenware; stoneware porringers are uncommon. This thick-walled and crudely fashioned piece, unmarked and undecorated, is probably from the late 18th or early 19th century. Collection of Mr. John Paul Remensnyder.

237. This small jar, about six inches high, is unusual in its handles, formed from two thin strips of clay twisted together to form a rope pattern before being pressed to the sides of the jar. The piece is unmarked and unidentified. The glaze is a rich and glossy brown-black slip, perhaps an Albany slip mixed with a manganese glaze. Collection of Mr. John Paul Remensnyder.

238. Much closer to the typical shape of red earthenware pieces of the 18th and 19th centuries, this stoneware porringer is more skill-fully made but hardly lighter than the piece in Plate 236. Like most such dishes, it is unmarked, and though certainly of the 19th century, essentially undatable. Rather than a clear salt glaze, the piece is covered inside and out, except for the base, in a reddish-brown Albany slip. Collection of Mr. John Paul Remensnyder.

239. The shape and form of mugs was nearly as constant over several centuries as that of porringers and other common wares. This unmarked piece, molded but hand finished, and dating probably from the 1890's or early 20th century, shows little substantive change from the Abraham Mead mug of 1773 (Plate 234). Collection of the author.

240. Taverns and restaurants, as they use marked dishes and glasses today, sometimes had marked stoneware beer and ale mugs made to order in quantity. If a customer carried one off, the deep stamp at least served as a perpetual advertisement. This mug, *c.* 1870–80, is decorated only with two bands of blue glaze and a stamp, "Atlantic Garden / 50 / Bowry," from New York City. Collection of Mr. John Paul Remensnyder.

241. Either the smallest cooler ever made or more likely a model or sample, this little container has a capacity of only one pint. Like the earlier Nathan Clark water cooler (Plate 241), it is completely enclosed—with the spigot hole as the only opening. The piece was made during 1840–42, and is marked "Dillon & Porter / Albany." The raised bands, to simulate barrel bands, were shaped with a sharp tool while the cooler turned on the potter's wheel. Blue glaze as well was applied by brush while the piece revolved. Albany Institute of History & Art.

242. Affectionately known as the Blind Pig, this most odd cooler holds a gallon of hard cider or beer. The flat or head end has a separately applied bushing to hold a wooden spigot, which would form a snout. The top filler-hole appears to be formed directly from the body; the four feet are separately applied. On a shelf, tail end out, the Blind Pig would certainly not appear as a dispenser for cider. The decoration of this piece is much less remarkable than its form, and consists entirely of brushed blue glaze banding and floral patterns, on all sides. It almost seems at times that the few potters with a really fine sense of humor preferred to remain anonymous, for like many other pieces in a similar vein, the Blind Pig is unmarked. Collection of Mr. John Paul Remensnyder.

243. This miniature churn, holding about three pints, was probably made not for household use, but for a druggist to mix liquid tonics and medicines. The purchaser's name is marked in blue script. Though the maker's mark is absent, the churn is known to be a product of Nathan Clark, Jr., of Athens, New York. The cover and plunger are wooden, though with these removed the churn might possibly have doubled as a druggist's mortar. New York State Historical Association.

244. Stoneware inkwells, generally quite simple, were made in all potteries. Of these three pieces, that on the left, decorated with incised and line-glazed birds and rabbits, is obviously an individual and special effort, though it is unmarked. The center example is a more typical production piece, and is marked by Clarkson Crolius, Jr., of New York City (1838–50). The mark is far more common than that on Plate 245. The right-hand inkwell, a mold-pressed piece, is remarkably similar to Plate 247, though simpler and from a different mold. This piece is marked only "Ink Fountain." Henry Ford Museum.

245. Marked pieces by Clarkson Crolius of New York City are among the rarest examples of stoneware, and small pieces even more so. This inkwell, pierced for four quill pens plus the recessed dipping well, is undecorated except for a thin band of blue glaze around the outside rim. It bears the mark of Clarkson Crolius, Sr., *c.* 1797–1815. The simplicity and lack of ornamentation would make it seem to have been a production piece rather than an individual one. Collection of Mr. John Paul Remensnyder.

246. This very unusual inkwell, with pen holders in the center, was probably made to hold two small glass liners—that for the ink on the right. The inkwell is decorated in blue glaze and is marked "C. P. T.," probably the person for whom it was made. The piece dates *c.* 1825–40. Henry Francis DuPont Winterthur Museum.

247. Certainly a specially made piece, this most elaborate inkwell is marked with the name "J. B. Cottle," probably the recipient rather than the maker. There is no other mark. Dated *c.* 1820–40, the inkwell seems to be an early example of pressing, in which clay was first pressed and formed inside a two–or four–section mold; the rough piece was then finished by hand on a wheel. The lettering and grooved and beaded bands are filled with blue glaze. Collection of Mr. John Paul Remensnyder.

248a–b. Writing with quills and India ink required sanders as well as inkwells. Such sanders, used in lieu of blotters, are sometimes mistakenly thought to be salt shakers. This sander (above), a single integral piece, was evidently made as a gift and is marked or inscribed on the base (right) "B. C. Miller / Maker / Sept. 1st, 1830 / W. H. Amos. [the recipient]." Henry Francis DuPont Winterthur Museum.

249. This desk sander, turned on a potter's wheel, was marked twice "Alexander & Coplin, Troy, 1829." Alexander & Coplin were not the makers, but rather the purchasers, who were probably dealers in dry goods and housewares. The lettering was filled with blue glaze, which was also brushed on the base and banding before the piece was fired and salt glazed. Albany Institute of History & Art.

250. Purely domestic objects in stoneware such as this salt shaker are most unusual. This piece was given its pie-crimped bands by hand, not a coggle wheel, and the crimpings were then filled with blue glaze. The shaker, c. 1860–80, is unmarked and its maker unknown. Henry Ford Museum.

251. Every pottery at one time or another produced stoneware flowerpots. This finely made and rather rococo example was first turned on a wheel. Then with a knife the potter split the edge of the pot and saucer, and with his fingers formed the double scalloping. The blue-glazed decoration of four-petaled flowers with stems passing through was basically a Pennsylvania-German design. This flowerpot's rope-turned handles are also suggestive of other pieces from eastern Ohio, an area to which many Pennsylvania potters migrated. Henry Francis DuPont Winterthur Museum.

252. An extremely unusual but very useful device was this chicken watering pot. The pot could be turned on its side and filled with water through the small hole in the inner base. Turned upright again, it would let water out only to the lower rim of the large outer hole, so that while chickens and other birds could drink, the water could never overflow. The chicken watering pot is formed in one piece and crudely painted with blue-glazed designs, as well as a small sprig of impressed leaves which seems to be a stamp. The piece is marked "Henry / Phila." Probably the name of the dealer rather then the maker. An identical piece is known marked by Thomas Haig of Philadelphia (1812–33). Henry Francis DuPont Winterthur Museum.

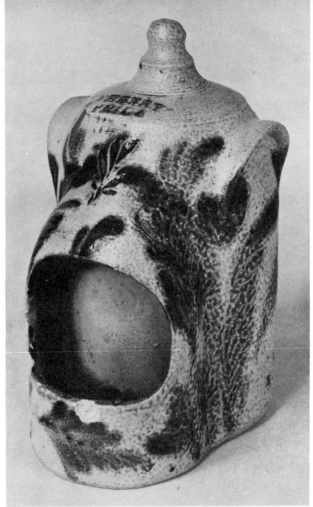

253. Whistles appealed particularly to Pennsylvania potters. Most were made of red earthenware. Blue decorated and salt-glazed stoneware whistles are quite rare. These three pieces, none marked, were molded, probably in some quantity. The tails of the roosters and the handle of the figure are mouthpieces. Henry Francis DuPont Winterthur Museum.

254. Commemorative medallions are extremely rare. These medallions, five inches in diameter, picture Queen Victoria and Prince Albert, and were probably made to commemorate their marriage in 1840. The medallions, however, are not English; they are attributed to the Nathan Clark Pottery of Athens, New York. As pressed or molded medallions, too, this pair was probably produced in some quantity. Collection of Mr. John Paul Remensnyder.

255. On occasion, strange things indeed were formed in stoneware. This flat piece, marked "H. R. Mitchell / Philadelphia," is probably a clock face, but a very strange one, for the numbering system follows no pattern, and certainly bears no relation to that of a standard clock. In addition, the compass map directions east, south, and west have been added. Henry Francis DuPont Winterthur Museum.

256, 257. These two salt-glazed banks, one with a single molded bird as a finial (256, right), the other with five (257, below), were made by Richard C. Remmey of Philadelphia in the mid-1880's. The single-finialed bank (Philadelphia Museum of Art) is marked in script "Anna Jamison"; the other (Henry Ford Museum), with floral incising, is marked "Giles B. Jamison / Bucks Co. / Phila. Nov. 12/86."

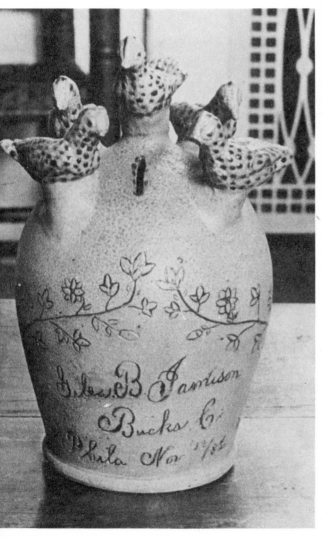

187

258. This little child's bank with a rope-turned handle was not marked, but was made in eastern Ohio, *c.* 1850. The outside is not salt glazed, but rather covered with a metallic, almost black Albany slip. Both the handle and glaze are very similar to the small jar in Plate 237. Donald Everhart Winer Museum.

259. Not a teapot but a child's bank, this little piece has a slot to take coins and is glazed outside with a brown Albany slip. The potter is unidentified; the marking "Office / Henry, Van Allen, Palmer..." is the name of the purchaser. The fact that the name is stamped indicates that these banks were probably purchased in quantity, perhaps as commercial gifts. Albany Institute of History & Art.

260. Figures of molded dogs, all directly derivative of the Staffordshire forms, were popular with all North American potters. This salt-glazed pair, with added blue-glazed fur, are very elaborate for American examples. Though no attribution is warranted, these figures are basically very similar to those in Plate 261. The smaller dog in the center, with simple blue-glazed spots is a much simpler, and a far more commonly found example; its maker is unknown. Henry Ford Museum.

261. As well as the simpler types, child's banks were made as well in unusual and artistic forms. Each of this pair of molded and salt-glazed dogs has a coin slot in its base. While the figures themselves are molded, the coloring is in blue glaze, and details such as the collars, tags, and leashes were done by hand incising. Though the exact origin of this pair is not known, the dogs were found in Hudson, New York, and are believed to have been made by the Nathan Clark Pottery in Athens, New York. Collection of Mr. John Paul Remensnyder.

262. This molded dog, again a child's bank, is not as elaborate as the previous pair. This figure is marked on the base "D. C. James / Greensboro," probably Pennsylvania, and dates c. 1860–80. Henry Francis DuPont Winterthur Museum.

263, 264, 265. Among the many forms which were once quite common but have now become extremely rare are simple miniature crocks and urns. In all possible details they duplicate the larger originals. Similar miniatures, from one to three inches in height, were once made by virtually every pottery in the Northeast. Some were intended as saltcellars; some were undoubtedly sample pieces; others were apprentice's exercises, and many were probably made as children's toys to be used in playing games or in furnishing large doll houses. That such pieces were made as common and familiar toys was indicative of the extent to which stoneware pottery was used in every American household. Henry Francis DuPont Winterthur Museum.

CHAPTER THIRTEEN

Bottles and Flasks

One group of salt-glazed stoneware utensils, produced in great quantity and variety during the 19th century, was rarely decorated in any way—bottles and flasks. Usually made in quart sizes, less commonly to hold a pint or two quarts, stoneware bottles filled a definite though limited need, but never became the sort of disposable container we think of in connection with even early glass bottles. In producing bottles, potteries faced a market situation that did not greatly affect other types of stoneware. Bottles made of pottery could not be manufactured in the same quantity or at the same speed and could not begin to compete with the far lower price of mass-produced glass bottles. Thus any liquid being sold in small units which remained on store shelves in individual containers was generally bottled in glass. Patent medicines, a huge industry after the Civil War, always came to the retailer and went to the consumer in glass bottles. Liquor, too, during the second half of the 19th century, was increasingly distributed in one-quart, brand-labeled glass

bottles rather than the earlier bulk containers. Household cleaners, druggists' prescriptions, and other items all were packaged in glass.

Stoneware bottles, however, had one definite advantage in a few specific markets in spite of expense (a dollar a dozen at the pottery) and weight—they insulated and kept liquids cold. The cost was lowered by continual refilling, while many glass bottles, particularly liquor and medicine bottles, were thrown away after use.

Thus the stoneware bottle was perfectly suited for beer and soft drinks, and particularly for use in taverns or stores where the customer wanted whatever he was drinking to be at least cool and preferably cold, in an age well before present-day forms of artificial refrigeration. Nothing was better on a hot summer day than a stoneware bottle of beer or sarsaparilla fresh from a cool dark cellar or underground storage area.

The great majority of stoneware bottles were made not for ultimate sale to individuals, but in quantity for brewers and soft drink producers, or on order for tavern keepers and store owners. These bottles were entirely utilitarian products rather than consumer commodities. They did not need, nor did they often have, the decoration so necessary for sales appeal on other consumer-oriented forms of stoneware.

Particularly in earlier periods, stoneware bottles were made in a variety of shapes, but after about 1850 for ease of manufacture almost all were produced with straight or slight tapered sides, with necks forming a cone and tapering to a heavy lip at the top. Nearly all were undecorated and many were completely unmarked. Others, however, were stamped on the wet clay with either the name of the pottery or, much more commonly, the name of the brewer, the soft drink bottler, the tavern or storekeeper who filled them from vats or barrels.

More rarely than the use of plain stamps, a little blue glaze came into play to alleviate the otherwise unbroken mass of gray pottery. The marking stamp might have been dipped in glaze which transferred the blue to the impressed lettering, or the marking may have been brushed with glaze. Occasionally a part of the bottle might have been colored as it turned on the potter's wheel—usually the formed lip or the conical neck. A few potters marked their initials or names in blue script. This, though, was about the extent of the decoration on most bottles, and none of it required the arts of a skilled decorator. Any boy could brush on a little glaze.

For today's collector the appeal of stoneware bottles lies not primarily in their elaborate decoration, which is rare indeed (though the collector always hopes), but in their shapes and variety of markings—individual and sometimes brand names such as "Guaranteed Sasparilla Beer," "Cronks Beer," and "Sparkling Gem."

Very occasionally the potters produced unique bottles—pieces of standard size but more finely shaped and formed, with incised or blue-glazed designs. Small, delicate, and thin-walled special purpose bottles were also made (perhaps for perfume or brandy), and these were often decorated as well. Bottles such as these were not a part of regular production, but were made as individual and unique pieces by potters for themselves or as gifts, or by senior apprentices as exercises and demonstrations of skill. Truly special and decorated bottles existing today are so rare that we can assume potters made very few. Perhaps it is because such pieces were difficult to form and fire, and were not particularly useful articles because of their fragility. To collectors, however, such bottles represent the pot at the end of the rainbow.

266. Potters in the early 19th century, before the universal acceptance of a cylindro-conical shape as the easiest to form mechanically, occasionally tried to duplicate in stoneware the shapes of glass bottles, successfully but probably slowly and with difficulty. This piece, *c.* 1810–30, in the accepted shape of a glass whisky or rum bottle, is unmarked, and like glass bottles was probably made to hold liquor. Collection of the author.

267. Here the potter has essentially duplicated the shape of a glass wine bottle, though with a needlessly heavy lip. This piece is also unmarked, though it was found in central New York State. Collection of the author.

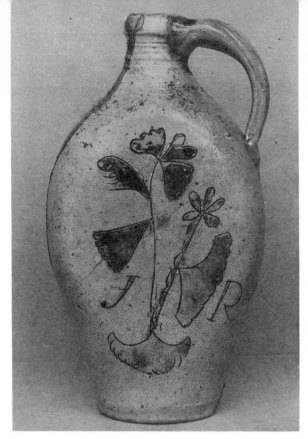

268. Another shape popular with pottery makers duplicated the flattened glass flasks of the 19th century. This handled flask bears an incised floral design on both sides, and has the typically banded neck of Hudson Valley and New York City pieces. The incised initials "J. R." suggest the piece might have been by John Remmey III of New York City. Henry Francis DuPont Winterthur Museum.

269. This flask is unidentified, but the blue design of two broken circles indicates James Morgan, Jr., (c. 1785–1805) of Cheesequake, New Jersey, as a possible maker. Collection of Mr. John Paul Remensnyder.

270. These tiny pieces, a Christmas-present flask and a handled bottle, are most unusual. The flask, with the heart and spelling indicating a Pennsylvania-German origin, is incised in script "John Marx / to / Arthur W. Smith / Dezember 25, / 1867." The handled bottle is decorated with a small incised and blue-glazed fish rather similar to that on the crock of Plate 170. Henry Ford Museum.

271. The most characteristic shape for post-1850 stoneware bottles resulted from the adoption of new machinery and processes for pressing or molding by nearly all bottle-making potteries. Though shapes varied somewhat, the slightly tapered cylindrical body was usually formed in one mold and the conical neck terminating in a heavy lip in another. The most common marking is a stamped name in printer's type, often with the stamp dipped in blue glaze to fill the lettering. The names on these bottles are those of quantity purchasers, not the makers. Collection of the author.

272. Decoration in blue cobalt, when it was used at all on later mass-produced bottles other than in stamps, usually appeared as a simple wash rather than a design. These bottles, marked respectively from the left "P. Mansfield" and "Gooding," have heavy lips coated with a thin brush-applied glaze. Collection of the author.

273, 274. Very occasionally bottles were marked in brushed or traced glaze rather than with a stamp. The "C. & P." (273, right) and "Post" (274, below) markings on these, like most stamped names, are merchants' marks (from the collections of the author and John Paul Remensnyder respectively). In this case, however, the bottles probably came from the Caire Pottery (1852–78) at Poughkeepsie, New York. Glazed markings are as unusual on bottles as they are common on larger pieces.

275. As well as individual names, brand names often appeared marked on stoneware bottles, but dated bottles are far more rare. This small piece, glazed with Albany slip, held about a pint of "Knickerbocker Porter." The date 1849 probably refers to when the brand was established, not to the date of the molded bottle. Collection of Mr. John Paul Remensnyder.

276. This unusual patent bottle with twelve sides and fluted neck is dated 1849 and marked "Patent / Pressed / W. Smith," the date being that of the molding process, not the bottle itself. Other twelve-sided bottles are known with the marks of Goodwin and Webster of Hartford, or Cowden and Wilcox of Harrisburg. The design was probably harder to press and finish than the plain cylindrical form, and never gained wide usage. Collection of John Paul Remensnyder.

277. This bottle, marked "Hiram Wheaton / 1873," had the entire neck, but not the body or lip, coated with blue glaze. Collection of Mr. John Paul Remensnyder.

278. With its simple but too heavily applied blue design, this flask, similar to other Pennsylvania pieces, once had a jug handle. Like most, it is unmarked. Handled flasks or bottles are most unusual in the United States, but were commonly made in Canada. Collection of Mr. John Paul Remensnyder.

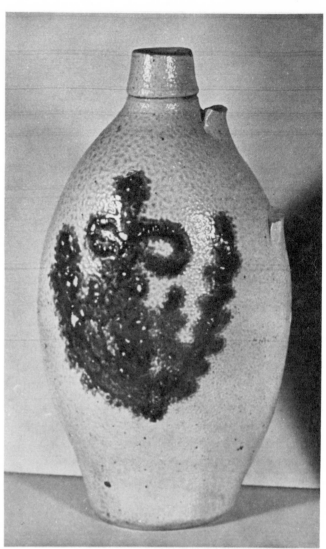

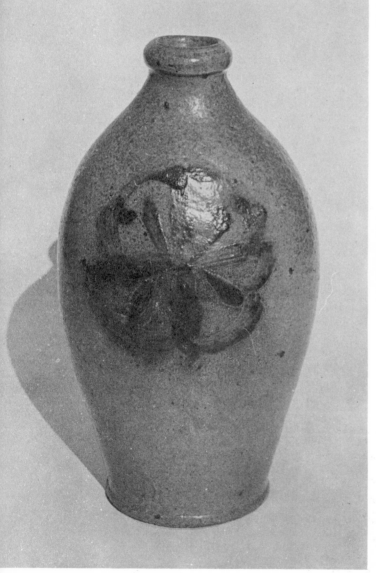

279. This very strange early 19th-century flask with a rapidly brushed flower in blue is unmarked, but could be of New York State origin. It was found in Utica, New York. The cross section is only slightly flattened—not nearly to the extent of most flasks. Collection of the author.

280. A pair of extremely fine flasks, one
has a rare molded decoration, the other
an incised ship. The flask on the left,
with a relief molding of a woman with
a wreath of flowers and fruit, is marked
"D. Rogers / 1855," either the owner or
an individual potter. The right-hand
piece shows a blue-glazed incised ship,
somewhat similar in treatment to those
in Plate 179a–b–c, and with its early
banded neck may be from the Morgan
or Warne & Letts Pottery in New
Jersey. Henry Ford Museum.

281. Elaborately incised with rare
intricacy, these flasks could be of
either Pennsylvania or New York
State origin. That on the left has a
fine grid design of perhaps a syca-
more leaf, with additional blue
surface decoration up the sides. The
decoration of a bird in a floral
wreath on the right-hand piece is
lined in blue. Henry Ford Museum.

199

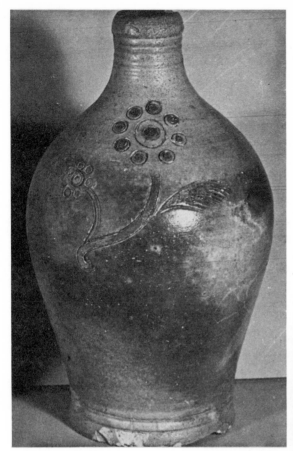

282, 283. Decorated miniature jugs used as vinegar cruets or bottles are most uncommon. These two pieces, both dating from the early 19th century, have simply incised floral designs lightly glazed in blue. Neither is marked, but both were probably made by New York City or New Jersey potteries. Collection of Mr. John Paul Remensnyder.

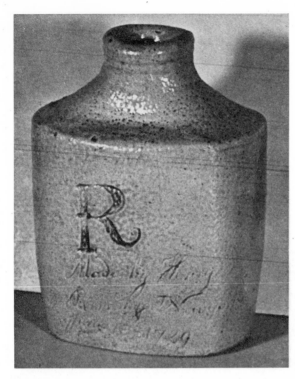

284. Among the rarest of all stoneware bottles are tiny pocket brandy or whisky flasks. This straight-sided piece is marked on one side with an incised "R" over an inscription "Made by Henry Remmy / New York / . . . 1789," and on the reverse side with a large incised "I. R." Henry Remmey may have been a member of the large New York pottery making family; the "I. R." marking suggests John Remmey II, who operated the pottery at that time. Collection of Mr. John Paul Remensnyder.

285. Another miniature flask, about four inches high, with the neck banding so commonly found on Hudson Valley pieces, was by an unidentified maker. The bottle is incised on one side "Catskill [N.Y.] / 1804," and the marking is somewhat obscured by a very light brushing of blue glaze. Collection of Mr. John Paul Remensnyder.

286. Almost like a perfume bottle, this little flask is round, about three and one half inches in diameter, and extremely flattened. It was probably formed on its side on a wheel, with the neck added as a separate piece. There are no identifying markings; the geometric design was incised on both sides, with alternate sections colored in blue. Collection of Mr. John Paul Remensnyder.

287. Probably a very small flower vase rather than a bottle, this unidentified piece with its simple swirls of blue has a very light, nearly white body. The essential shape is still as popular as it must have been when this piece was made, *c.* 1850; in silhouette, the vase could be contemporary. Collection of Mr. John Paul Remensnyder.

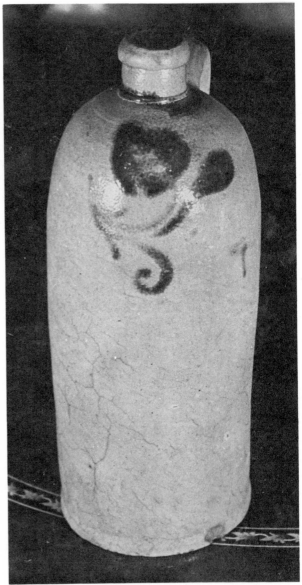

288. Brandy bottles of this shape are commonly found with a very dark salt glaze, usually of a fairly recent Portuguese or Dutch manufacture and so marked. This bottle, however, is unquestionably American from the mid-19th century, with a simple blue floral design and a light-colored body. Collection of Mr. John Paul Remensnyder.

289. Either a large-necked bottle of about one-quart size, or a small-necked jar, this bottle has the surface brushed-glazed design of a Germanic tulip. The piece is unmarked, though it is of Canada West origin, and was probably a product of Eberhardt of Toronto or of the Brantford, Ontario Pottery. Metropolitan Toronto & Region Conservation Authority.

290. Over-the-shoulder or harvest canteens were probably an occasional product of many potters, and a number of such pieces are known. Filled with water, they were meant to be carried with arm and shoulder through the central hole, an ill-fitting and uncomfortable arrangement at best. Most such known canteens, though, are of red earthenware coated with a lead oxide glaze; this canteen of salt-glazed stoneware is extremely rare and may well be unique. Collection of Mr. John Paul Remensnyder.

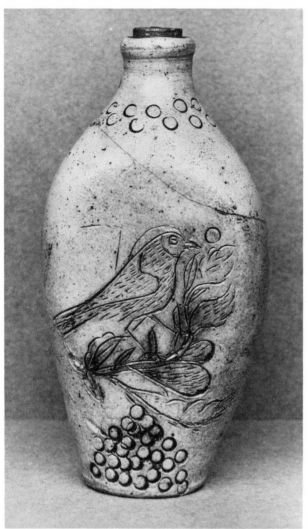

291. Another elaborately decorated and unusual bottle, this flask is incised with a somewhat crudely done but quite detailed bird. It is standing on a bush limb, with small incised lines within both; the lines are filled with blue glaze. Though the maker is unidentified, the flask is similar to other Pennsylvania pieces in its elongated shape and slightly rolled neck. Henry Francis DuPont Winterthur Museum.

292. The headless turtle is certainly one of the most unusual stoneware bottles or flasks ever to appear; the top and base shells form the actual body of the piece. It is impossible to tell whether the flask was shaped in a mold; perhaps the parts were, but there are no visible seams except where the neck was applied, and a mold would have had to be broken to remove such a casting. More unlikely the turtle was an exercise by an unknown but extremely skilled potter-sculptor, but the piece is unmarked. The shell neck and body are decorated with a blue surface glaze, and the piece probably dates from the second quarter of the 19th century. Collection of Mr. John Paul Remensnyder.

CHAPTER FOURTEEN

Billheads and Price Lists

In doing any sort of investigation of North American 18th- and 19th-century pottery there are usually three avenues of approach —examination of existing examples in quantity, documentary research, and archaeology. The pottery itself we have now examined in the earlier chapters; but like every other industry every pottery, besides producing stoneware, generated documents —price lists and order forms, letterheads, advertising cards, account books, and so on. Manuscript material was, of course, unique and purely for internal use. Printed material originally was for distribution, but was largely of the temporary interest and throwaway type, and thus little is still extant.

The pottery itself as we see it in museums and private collections cannot tell us everything we need to know. The objects alone give us no idea of the full range of any particular pottery's production, or of prices or dates of various pieces. Thus for any research in depth it becomes essential to locate and explore extant documents that focus on particular potteries or areas.

Perhaps the single most valuable form of printed matter is the price list and order form, once distributed by the thousands by virtually every stoneware pottery. Customarily these order forms were printed on a single sheet, listing the full line of a pottery's standard or stock production, with prices of the pottery for dozen lots and sometimes for single pieces. Most order forms still surviving are dated, and many have been filled out so that they offer a sharp vignette not only of what was available at a specific time but often what was most commonly bought and sold by retail dealers. Orders filled in usually indicate the same basic pottery types that are still most commonly seen today— jugs, crocks, churns, and general containers. The order forms of most potteries, however, also generally list numbers of articles (utensils rather than storage containers) which are rarely if ever encountered today, and in all likelihood were made in very small quantity on scattered occasions. The smaller pieces, too, are doubly difficult to pin down and identify as to origin even when they are found, since, unlike the jugs and crocks, few were ever marked.

From Thomas Chollar's handsome handbill of about 1840 (Plate 293), what has become of the listed one- and two-quart pitchers, the spitoons, the soap dishes, and the inkwells? Where are the Clark and Fox salt-glazed mugs, snuff jars, medicine jars, and wash bowls, all listed in 1837? In a great many cases we find items listed which could be suspected of never having been made at all, though conversely, we can occasionally find existing marked pieces which never appeared on the lists. In other cases, archaeological digging will confirm or supplement listings. Recent excavations at Brantford, Ontario, have unearthed dozens of small intact inkwells, all unmarked, and previously quite unknown.

Price lists and order forms, in spite of sometimes questionable reliability, still offer today as complete a documentary picture of product variety as can be had. Occasionally, too, these forms will bear a contemporary wood or steel engraving of the pottery itself, witness the Norton of Bennington order form of the 1850's (Plate 296). Correspondence letterheads also are often found with small illustrations.

Stoneware potteries were usually not big advertisers. Neither were they habitual subscribers to city directories, county atlases, or county histories, in which, of course, the paying subscribers generally received the greatest and most favorable mention. Faced with intense competition from other producers as well as substitute products, stoneware potteries were not notoriously lucrative enterprises, and what little advertising they did was logically directed toward retailers, not individual consumers. Thus it is not uncommon to find some large potteries which were major local industries but which were non-advertisers, receiving only the barest mention in directories and in local newspapers.

The documentary research essential to trace in reliable detail the span of any pottery is often frustrating in its results, for the task usually involves the bit-by-bit compilation of small pieces of information—a directory advertisement here, an order form there, the occasional recorded property transfer, and so on. The whole picture emerges only slowly, and still a great deal is usually lacking.

The printed remnants of pottery operations, or of any early industry, are in many ways more valuable than the pieces of pottery themselves, primarily because of their information, but to collectors and libraries often because of their own rarity. For a purely object-oriented study, order forms and billheads alone can offer overviews of pottery production, confirm finds from excavations, or give a picture of prices and the economics of stoneware manufacture. As nothing else, in fact, early price lists in progression over the years illustrate very clearly the economic effects of the trend in stoneware making from craft to machine, and point to the reasons for the eventual failure of all but the strongest producers.

From the seven price lists illustrated, in 1837 Clark and Fox priced four-gallon pots and jugs at standard pieces of $.54 each or $6.48 a dozen. Thomas Chollar in 1840 listed the same pieces at $7.50 for four-gallon pots, and $6.50 a dozen for three-gallon jugs. By 1852 the Nortons at Bennington listed four-gallon pots and jugs at $8.00 a dozen. Then from the middle '50's through the 1870's by virtue of industry agreements prices stabilized at a yet higher level. The Albany Stoneware Factory in the late 1850's, Charles Hart in 1865, and the Russells at West Troy in 1875 all listed the same four-gallon jugs and pots without covers at $10.00 a dozen. All production of this period was still from hand operations and relatively small potteries.

Then entered the new technology, dependent on an accumulation of capital that was simply not possible for the small and individually owned operation.

The 1899 list of the Syracuse Stoneware Company presents the new picture vividly. The Syracuse company offered a wide variety of articles, pressed or slip-cast. All items were eminently practical but certainly without decorative or aesthetic appeal; they were made by machines, not potters. With eleven factories, undoubtedly a staggering productive capacity, and all the advantages of capital and technology, four-gallon jugs were offered at $3.84 per dozen; uncovered four-gallon pots at $3.12. For other similar products as well, prices had reduced in equal proportions from earlier levels.

While the consumer obviously benefited, the individual manufacturer with his few employees and handmade products was finished forever. We cannot today, however, lament the passing of a defunct craft. Had pottery always been a product of technology, or if salt-glazed pottery was even today a universal product of a craft, we would have little interest in it from either an object study or historical viewpoint. The fact that stoneware pottery making *was* a craft and that it is very much of the past is the essence of its contemporary appeal and value.

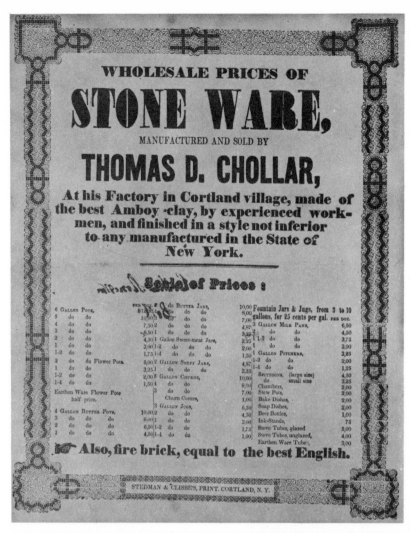

293. Thomas Chollar, who began making stoneware at Cortland, New York, in 1837, distributed this broadside listing wares in about 1840. Like most stoneware potteries, Chollar's factory made a few products of local red earthenware clay as well. Broome County Historical Society.

294. While never as completely informative as price lists, directory advertisements were very often useful in the absence of anything better. This advertisement of Hubbell and Chesebro of Geddes, New York offers simply a general idea of what was produced. Onondaga County Historical Society.

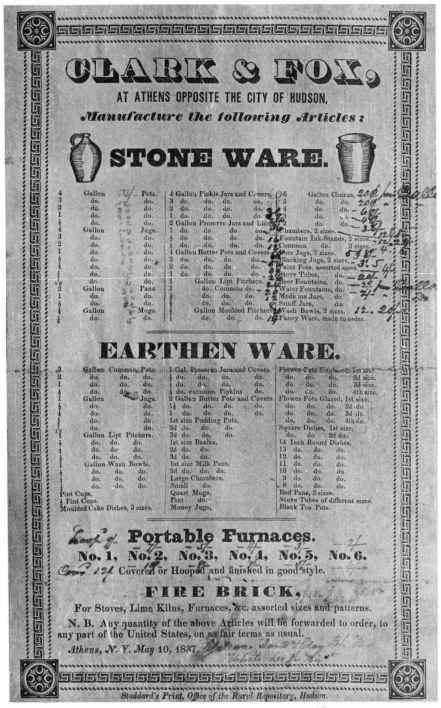

295. The partnership of Nathan Clark, Jr., and E. S. Fox operated the great Clark Pottery (1805–92) at Athens, New York, 1829–38. Their handbill of 1837 was probably published strictly as an advertising piece; here price per unit has been entered by hand. Note that the Clark Pottery stocked pint and half-pint jugs and mugs (very rare today) as well as "Fancy Ware, made to order," and a whole range of red earthenware. New York State Historical Association.

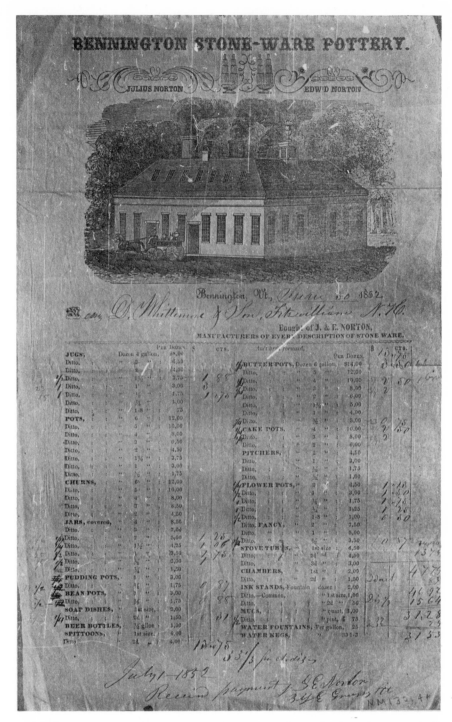

296. The Bennington Stoneware Pottery was perhaps the best known of all stoneware manufacturers. In the early 1850's it published this combined price list and order form, which included a wood engraving of the factory. This list includes only salt-glazed stoneware, and there are fewer unusual or smaller utensils listed than were actually being made. New York State Historical Association.

ALBANY
STONEWARE FACTORY.

Albany, 185_

M_____

Bought of M. A. STAUDINGER.

Jugs.		Retail DOLLS CTS.				Butter Pots, Covered.		Retail DOLLS CTS.	
	PER DOZEN.					*Amount brot forward.*			
Doz. 4 Gallon,	$10 00	$0 85					PER DOZEN.		
3 "	8 00	69				Doz. 6 Gallon,	$16 00	$1 37
2 "	6 00	50				5 "	14 00	1 18
1 1-2 "	4 50	37				4 "	12 00	1 00
1 "	3 50	31				3 "	9 50	81
1-2 "	2 50	25				2 "	7 00	63
1-4 "	1 50	18				1 1-2 "	5 75	47
1-8 "	1 00	9				1 "	4 50	38
Pots without Covers.						1-2 "	3 50	31
Doz. 6 Gallon,	$14 00	$1 18				1-4 "	2 50	19
5 "	11 00	94				**Cake Pots, Covered.**		
4 "	10 00	85				Doz. 4 Gallon,	$12 00	$1 00
3 "	8 00	69				3 "	9 50	81
2 "	6 00	56				2 "	7 00	63
1 1-2 "	4 50	37				**Pitchers.**		
1 "	3 50	31				Doz. 2 Gallon,	$6 00	$0 50
1-2 "	2 50	25				1 1-2 "	4 50	37
1-4 "	quart pots, 1	5				1 "	3 50	31
Preserve Jars, Covered.						1-2 "	2 50	25
Doz. 4 Gallon,	$10 00	$0 85				1 1 "	1 50	13
3 "	8 00	69				**Flower Pots.**		
2 "	6 00	50				Doz. 2 Gallon,	$5 50	$0 50
1 1-2 "	5 00	42				1 "	3 50	31
1 "	4 00	35				1-2 "	2 50	25
1-2 "	2 75	25				1-4 "	1 75	15
1-4 "	1 75	15				1-8 "	1 00	9
Churns.						**Chambers.**		
Doz. 6 Gallon,	$15 00	$1 25				Doz. 1st size,	$3 50	$0 31
5 "	13 00	1 00				2d "	2 50	31
4 "	11 00	94				**Spittoons.**		
3 "	9 00	75				Bar Room Spittoons,	$9 00	$0 75
2 "	7 00	62				Doz. 1st size	6 00	50
Pudding Pots.						2d "	4 50	38
Doz. 1 Gallon,	$3 50	$0 31				**Water Fountains.**		
1-2 "	2 50	25				Per Gallon,	$0 25	
Bean Pots.						**Water Kegs.**		
Doz. 1 Gallon,	$3 50	$0 31				Per Gallon,	$0 44	
1-1 "	2 50	25				**Soap Dishes.**		
Mugs.						Doz. 1-1 size,	$2 00	$0 17
Doz. Quart,	$1 25	$1 11				2d "	1 50	12
Pint,	1 00	9				**Beer Bottles.**		
Molasses Jugs.						Doz. 1-4 Gallon,	$1 25	
Doz. 2 Gallon,	$6 50	$0 56				**Stove Tubes.**		
1 "	4 00	38				Doz. Assorted,	$3 00	
1-2 "	2 75	25						

Orders by Mail are respectfully solicited, and punctually executed.

Received Payment

297. The Albany Stoneware Factory, Albany, New York, which operated under a succession of proprietors, in the 1850's offered only quite standard pieces. The prices of stock stoneware articles in dozen lots by the middle of the '50's had risen considerably from those in the 1830's. From then on, however, prices were stabilized, and following a general pottery industry agreement in 1863, virtually all stoneware producers held to the same price structure. New York State Historical Association.

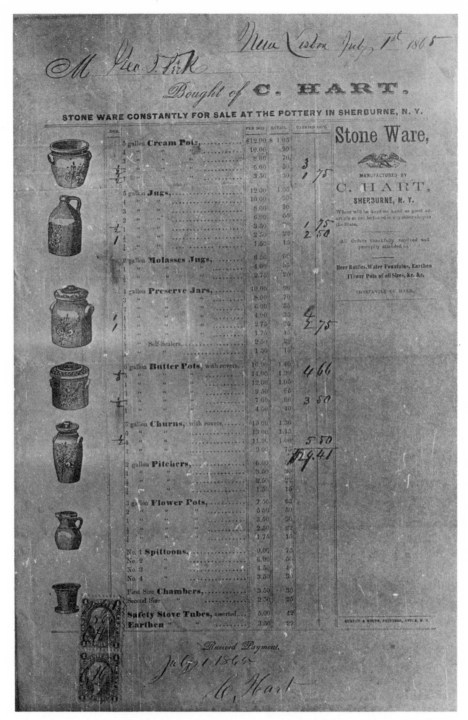

298. Charles Hart, who had been in partnership with his father in Sherburne, New York, since 1841, operated his own pottery at Ogdensburg from 1850–58 and then returned to Sherburne. This combination price list and order form of 1865 offers only basic articles. The small illustrations were probably standard printers' cuts, and did not necessarily reflect the actual shape or decoration of the pottery being made. New York State Historical Association.

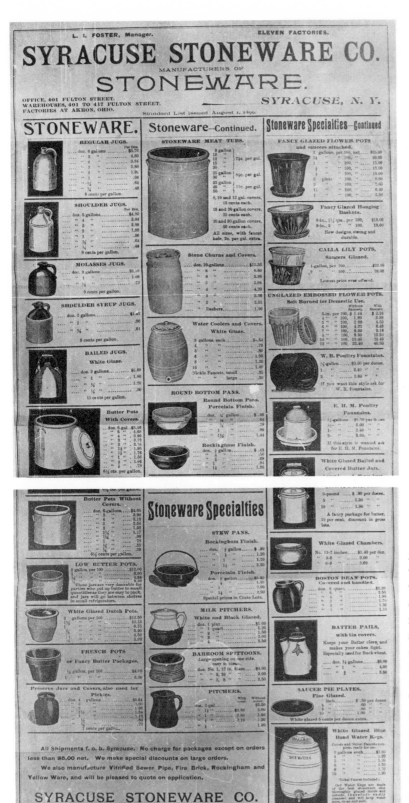

299a–b. By the early 1900's, stoneware was still being produced in a vast range of articles, but it had come to be a product of machines rather than of men, quite lacking in any sign of hand craftsmanship or decoration. This list of the Syracuse Stoneware Co., published in 1899, offers a vast range of products. The technological revolution that forced virtually all small potteries out of existence is clearly evident in the price reductions even after 1875. No producer dependent on the hand labor of craftsmen was able to compete. New York State Historical Association.

213

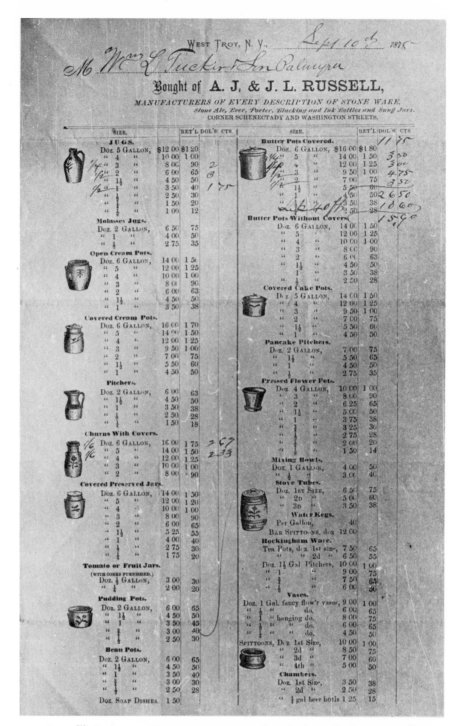

300. Russell's Pottery at West Troy, New York, which marked its pieces "West Troy Pottery," was producing a full range in 1875. Like most potteries, Russell's did not list everything they made; note the heading "Manufacturers of . . . Ale, Beer, Porter, Blacking and Ink Bottles and Snuff Jars," none of which could really be ordered on this form. New York State Historical Association.

A Checklist of Potteries

It might be well to point out, initially, that in the 18th and 19th centuries stoneware potteries were never as numerous as potteries producing utensils in red earthenware. Because of the ease of utilizing local clays and firing pottery at lower temperatures, in many areas of the U.S. redware producers were often active in a numerical proportion of six to one or more over stoneware makers, who needed both imported clays and a more sophisticated physical establishment. In eastern Canada, where stoneware manufacturing was late in coming, and always faced U.S. and British competition, the ratio of earthenware to stoneware potteries was more often 12 or even 20 to 1.

This checklist, then, includes only known salt-glazed stoneware (not earthenware) potters and pottery proprietors of the 18th to 20th centuries—the people or firms that marked or could have marked their products. There has been no attempt to include the individual employees who worked in various pottery establ'shments, but were never partners, managers, or proprietors.

At the present time, no checklist of this type of stoneware potteries could conceivably be called complete, for in many geographical areas little or no previous work has been done on early potters. In other cases what previous publications exist may be quite old, and originally incomplete. In general, the areas where the most research has been done and the early potteries are hence best established and known are New England, New York, New Jersey, Ontario, and Quebec. Less complete is knowledge of pottery operations in the Middle Atlantic States and the Midwest. Very little work, then, has been done on the Southern and Western United States or the Canadian maritime provinces.

The primary entries in the listing, not marked by an asterisk, are from greatly varied specific sources, including both recent publications and early business directories, advertising, town and county histories, and census enumerations. Datings have been checked as closely as possible, and markings are included from personal ob-

215

servation. (An absence of mention of markings for various potters means only that marks have not been seen personally.)

Those entries preceded by an asterisk are from the checklist in Ramsay, *American Potters and Pottery*, 1939. This listing is the most extensive ever published, and has never been republished, but it is also often unreliable, particularly in citations of dates of operation. Entries from Ramsay have been included and marked with an asterisk here for some states where no other information was available, and none have been separately confirmed.

Obviously not all stoneware potteries that once operated are known today, and so too, a few are known only to have existed, without other information. These must ultimately be added to the list.

*Abbe, Frederick, Columbus, O., c. 1848–50.
*Adams Bros., East Liverpool, O., 1856–72.
Adley, G., & Co., Ithaca, N.Y., c. 1860–80.
  Mark, name and address impressed.
Ahrens, Jacob H., Paris, Ont., c. 1848–83.
  Mark, name and address impressed.
*W. B. Allison & Co., Middlebury, Akron, O., c. 1865–75.
  Allison & Hart, c. 1875–80.
*Amos, William, Baltimore, Md., 1833–37.
*Anderson, William A., Anderson's Landing, Pa., c. 1870–80.
  Mark, name and address stenciled.
Armstrong & Wentworth, Norwich, Ct., 1814–34.
*Atcheson, H. S., Annapolis, Ind., 1841–1900.
*Atwater, Caleb and Joshua, Atwater (and Atwater Station), O., c. 1830–40.
*Auber, P., Birmingham, Pa., c. 1860.

*Bagnall, George, Newcomerstown, O., c. 1870–75.
*Bakewell, H. N., Wellsburg, W. Va., c. 1831–41.
*Balderson & Pace, Roseville, O., c. 1875.
Ballard, H. N., O. L. & A. K., Burlington, Vt., 1856–72.
  Marks varied and address impressed.
*Batchelder Pottery, Menasha, Wis., c. 1850–80.
*Bauders, F., Pittsburgh, Pa., c. 1841.
*Beckting Bros., Huntingburg, Ind., c. 1870–1900.
*Beckting Bros., Evansville, Ind., 1885–1900.
*Beecher & Lantz, Akron, O., 1863–c. 83.
*Bell, John, Waynesboro, Pa., 1833–81.
  Mark, name or name and address impressed.
*Bell, Joseph, Putnam O., 1827–50.
  Mark, name impressed.
*Bennett, Edwin, Baltimore, Md., 1846–49.
  E. & W. Bennett, 1849–56.
Bertrand & Lavoie, Iberville, Que., c. 1885–c. 95.
  Mark, name and address impressed.
*Binkley, George, Canton, O., 1826–c. 40.
  Mark, "B" impressed.
Bissett, Asher, Old Bridge, N.J., 1800–1815.
  Bissett, Evert & D., 1815–60.
Blair, Sylvester, Cortland, N. Y., 1829–35.
  Mark, name and address impressed.
*Bodenbuhl, Peter, Akron, O., c. 1863–70.
*Bodine, J., Putnam, O., c. 1836–45.
*Boerner, Shapley & Vogt, Massillon Stoneware Co., Massillon, O., 1882–1900.
Boone, Benjamin, Brooklyn, N.Y., 1846–63.
  Boone, Thomas, E., 1858–64.
Boone, T. G., Brooklyn, N.Y., 1839–46.
  Mark, name and address impressed.
  After 1842, T. G. Boone & Sons.
*Booth Bros., East Liverpool, O., c. 1858–65.
*Boss Bros., Akron, O., c. 1874.
  Mark, name and address impressed.
Boston Pottery Co., Boston, Mass., 1878–c. 1900.
  Mark, name and address impressed.
Bowne, Catherine, Cheesequake, N.J., 1815–39.
*Boynton, C., & Co., Troy, N.Y., c. 1860.
*Boynton, . . . , Red Wing, Minn., 1870–72.
Boynton & Farrar, St. Albans, Vt., c. 1860.
  Mark, name and address impressed.
Brantford Stone Ware Manufacturing Co., Brantford, Ont., 1894–1907.
  Mark, name and address impressed.

Braun, C. W., Buffalo, N.Y., *c.* 1860.

Brayton, Kellogg & Doolittle, Utica, N.Y., 1827–*c.* 40.

Brickner, John, Albany, N.Y., 1842–48 with E. Orcutt; independent 1848–55.

Briggs, John H., Lew-Beach, N.Y., *c.* 1850–60.
Mark, name and address impressed.

*Bromley, William, Cincinnati, O., 1843–60.
Bromley & Son, 1860–*c.* 70.

*Broome & Morgan, Dayton, O., 1882–*c.* 1900.

Brown Brothers, Huntington (L.I.), N.Y., 1863–1904.
Mark, name and address impressed.
Brown, S. C., 1863–1904.
Mark, name and address impressed.

*Brown, S. H., Harmony, Ind., *c.* 1869–1900.

*Brown & McKenzie, East River, W. Va., *c.* 1870–90.

Bruer, Stephen T., New London, Ct., 1828–30.
Mark, name and address impressed.
Pottery operated 1800–1832; stoneware known only by Bruer.

*Buchanan, Thomas, Columbus, O., *c.* 1850.

Bullard, Joseph O. & Scott, Alexander F., Allston, Mass., *c.* 1870–1909.
Marks, name and varied addresses.

*Bullock, W., Roseville, O., *c.* 1870–85.
Mark, name and address impressed.

*Burchfield, A. N., Pittsburgh, Pa., *c.* 1860.

Burger, John, Rochester, N.Y., *c.* 1860.
Mark, name and address impressed.

*Burgess, Webster & Viney, East Liverpool, O., 1867–69.

*Burley, John, Mount Sterling, O., *c.* 1840–50.

*Burley, Lazalier, Crooksville, O., *c.* 1846.

*Burley & Winters, Crooksville, O., *c.* 1850–90.
Mark on brownware, name and address impressed.

Burney, J. M., Jordan, N.Y., *c.* 1850–60.
Mark, name (later "& Son") and address impressed.

Burns, James R. & Campbell, . . . , Toronto Ont. *c.* 1871–*c.* 90.
Mark, name and address impressed.

*Burns, W. F., Atwater Station, Atwater, O.. 1850–74.

*Burton, John, Roseville, O., *c.* 1887.

*Butler A. J., & Co., New Brunswick, N.J., *c.* 1850.
Mark, name and address impressed.

Caire, Frederick J., Huntington (L. I.), N.Y., 1854–63.
Mark, name and address impressed.

Caire, John P., Poughkeepsie, N.Y., 1840–42.
Caire, Jacob, 1842–52.

*Callahan, William, Martin's Ferry, O., *c.* 1837.

*Camp, Cook & Co., Cuyahoga Falls, O., 1863–*c.* 80.

*Camp & Thomson, Akron, O., *c.* 1870–80.
Mark, name impressed.

Campbell, Justin, Utica, N.Y., 1826–*c.* 40.
Mark, name and address impressed.

*Canfield, . . . , Milford Center, O., 1857–69.

Capron, William, Albany, N.Y., 1800–*c.* 1808.

*Carlyle & McFadden, Freeman's Landing, W. Va., 1850–53.

Carpenter, Frederick, possibly Boston, Mass., 1801–12.
At Edmands Pottery, 1812–27.

Central New York Pottery Co., Utica, N.Y., *c.* 1875–1900.

Chace, Leonard, Benjamin, & Clark, Pottersville (Somerset), Mass., *c.* 1845–82; *see* Somerset Pottery.

Chapman, Josiah, Troy, N.Y., *c.* 1810–19.
Mark, "J. Chapman/Troy/Factory."

Chollar, Thomas, Cortland, N.Y., 1832–42.
Chollar & Bennett, 1842–44.
Chollar & Darby, 1844–49.
Marks, name and "Cortland" or "Homer" (N.Y.).

Clark, J., Troy, N.Y., *c.* 1840.
Mark, name and address impressed.

Clark, Nathan, Athens, N.Y., as:
Howe & Clark, 1805–13.
Nathan Clark, 1813–29.
Clark & Fox, 1829–38.
E. S. Fox, 1838–43.
Nathan Clark, Jr., 1843–92.
Marks, names and addresses. Subsidiary at Lyons, N.Y., *c.* 1825–52; at Mt. Morris, *c.* 1825–*c.* 40.

Clough, Calhoun & Co., Portland, Maine, 1847–48.
Mark, name and address impressed.

Columbian Pottery, Perth Amboy, N.J. (Stockwell, Henry & Warner, William E.), *c.* 1830–35.
Mark, names and address impressed.

Commeraw, Thomas, New York City, 1795–97, 1802–12, 1815–20.

Mark, "COMMERAWS/STONEWARE/CORLEARS/ HOOK/N.YORK."

Congress Pottery, South Amboy, N.J., 1828–c. 54.

Hancock, William H., 1828–40.
Mark, name impressed.

Price, G., 1840–49.

Cadmus, Abraham, 1840–c. 54.

*Cook & Richardson, Akron, O., 1869–c. 80.

Cook, Fairbanks & Co., c. 1880–87.

Cowden & Wilcox, Harrisburg, Pa., c. 1870–90.
Mark, name and address impressed.

Crafts, Caleb, Whately, Mass., c. 1815–20.

Troy, N.Y., c. 1820–37.

Portland, Maine, 1837–43.

Nashua, N.H., 1843–45.

Whately, Mass., 1845–54.
Mark, "C. Crafts & Co."

Crafts, Edward, A.; see Wells.

Crafts, Martin, trained Whately, Mass., Portland, Maine, 1834–39.

Nashua, N.H., 1839–51 (pottery closed 1852).
Mark varied, "M. Crafts & Co." and addresses.

Whately, Mass., 1857–61.
Marks varied, name and address impressed.

Crafts, Thomas, Whately, Mass., 1833–48.

James M., 1848–61.
Marks, names and address impressed.

*Crock, Charles, Santa Fe, Ill., c. 1880.

Crolius, Clarkson (Sr.), New York City, 1794–1837.
Mark varied, name and address impressed.

Crolius, Clarkson, Jr., New York City, 1838–50.
Mark, name and address impressed.

Crolius, John, New York City, late 18th century.

Crolius, William & Remmey, John, New York City, pre-1735–c. 60.

Cross, Peter, Hartford, Ct., 1805–18.

Cushman, Paul, Albany, N.Y., 1809–32.
Marks, name only or "PAUL CUSHMAN STONEWARE FACTORY: ONE MILE EAST OF THE ALBANY GAOL."

Darrow, John, Baldwinsville, N.Y., 1860–74.
Marks, name only or name and address (later "& Sons"), impressed.

Devol & Catterson, Shoals, Ind., c. 1870.

*Dick, Jacob, Tuscarawas Co., O., exact location unknown, c. 1830–40.

Mark, name and county impressed.

Dillon, Charles, Albany, N.Y., c. 1825–42.

Tyler & Dillon, 1827–34.

C. Dillon & Co., 1833–40.

Dillon & Porter, 1840–42.
Marks, names and address.

*Donahue Pottery, Parkersburg, W. Va., 1874–1900.

*Donaldson, Hugh, Pittsburgh, Pa., c. 1839.

Dorchester Pottery Works, Dorchester, Mass., c. 1880.

*Dunscombe, Hannah, Warren Co., O., exact location unknown, c. 1850.

*Dyke & Co., A. L., Akron, O., 1884–91.

*Dyke & Co., Samuel, Akron, O., 1889–91.

*Eagle Pottery Co., Macomb, Ill., c. 1880–91.

Eaton, Jacob & Stout, Samuel, Washington, N.J., 1818–45.
Mark, names and address impressed.

Eberhardt, N. Toronto, Ont., 1866–?
Mark, name and address impressed.

*Economy Society Pottery, Beaver Falls, Pa., c. 1834–81.

Edmands, Barnabas & Burroughs, William, Charlestown, Mass., 1812–50.

Emands & Co., 1850–c. 65.

Powers & Edmands, 1868.

Edmands & Hooper, to 1905.
Marks, names and address impressed.

*Eichenlaub, Valentine, Cincinnati, O., 1855–57.

*Eichert, Peter and Fleckinger, Jacob, Orrville, O., 1877–1900.

*Elverson & Sherwood, New Brighton, Pa., c. 1870.

Sherwood Bros. Co., 1877–1900.

*Emsinger, A., Jonathan Creek, O., c. 1828–40.

*Enterprise Pottery Co., Fallston, Pa., c. 1880–1900.

*Euler & Sunshine, Pittsburgh, Pa., c. 1860.

*Fallston Pottery Co., Fallston, Pa., c. 1875–1900.

*Farrar, Ebenezer L., Burlington, Vt., c. 1850–71.
Mark, name and Fairfax or Burlington address impressed.

Farrar, Isaac Brown, Fairfax, Vt., c. 1815–38.

George W. & J. H. Farrar, 1838–c. 55.

Farrar, Moses, St. Johns, Que., c. 1840–c. 45.

Farrar & Soule, Warren, c. 1846–c. 55.

E. L. & G. W. Farrar, c. 1855–56.

Farrar, G. W., c. 1855–71.

G. H. & L. E. Farrar, 1871–c. 80.

G. H. Farrar, Iberville, Que., c. 1880–1927.
Varied marks, names and addresses impressed.

Farrar & Stearns, Fairfax, Vt., 1851–52.
Mark, name and address impressed.

Farrar, Williams H., Geddes (Syracuse), N.Y., 1841–58. Relocated at Syracuse 1858–71.
Mark, name and address impressed.

Farrington, E. W., Elmira, N.Y., c. 1880.
Mark, name and address impressed.

Fayette, Shavalia, Utica, New York, c. 1832.
Mark, name and address impressed.

Fenton, Jacob, New Haven, Ct., c. 1790–1801. Burlington, N.Y., after 1801.

Fenton, Jonathan, Boston, Mass., 1794–96. Walpole, N. H., 1797–1801. Dorset, Vt., 1801–c. 40.

*Fenton, J. H., Mogadore, O., c. 1854–75.

Fenton, Richard Webber, St. Johnsbury, Vt., 1808–59.
Marks varied, names and address impressed.

*Fenton, T. H., Tallmadge, O., c. 1850–80.

*Figley, Joseph, New Philadelphia, O., c. 1850.
Mark, "J. Figley" impressed.

*Fish, C., Swan Hill Pottery, South Amboy, N.J., 1849–50.

Fisher, Jacob, Hartford, Ct., c. 1805.

Fisher, Jacob, Lyons, N.Y., 1872–c. 1900.
Mark, name and address impressed.

*Fisher, John, Cambria Co., Pa., exact location unknown, c. 1879.

*Fisher & McLain, Hillsboro, O., c. 1810–40.

*Fisher, Thomas, Steubenville, O., 1808–c. 25.

*Fisher & Tarr (Thos. Fisher), Steubenville, O., c. 1820.

*Fiske & Smith, Springfield (now part of Akron), O. c. 1822–30.

Flack, David & Van Arsdale, Isaac, Cornwall, Ont., c. 1861–c. 1905.
Mark, name and address impressed, or "Cornwall Pottery."

*Foel & Ault, E. Birmingham, Pa., c. 1860.

Fort Edward Pottery Co., Fort Edward, N.Y., c. 1870–80.
Mark, name and address impressed.

*Fossbender, N., Mogadore, O., 1860–75.

*Fowler & McKenzie, Vanport, Pa., 1870–1900.

Fox, E. S., Athens, N.Y., 1838–43; *see* Clark, N.

*Fox, Harmon and Gustavus, Newcomerstown, O., 1840–c. 60.

*Frell, John & Co., Pittsburgh, Pa., c. 1860.

*French, Eben, Chatfield Corners, O., c. 1837–45.

Fulper, Abraham, Flemington, N.J., 1805–? Stoneware only after c. 1840. Later Fulper Bros., and Fulper Pottery (present).
Marks varied, name and address impressed.

Furman, Noah, South Amboy, N.J., 1846–56.
Mark, name and address impressed.

Gay, Amos, Utica, N.Y., c. 1829.
Mark, name and address impressed.

Geddes Stone Ware Pottery Co., Geddes (Syracuse), N.Y., 1883–87.

*Getz, . . . , Dayton, O., c. 1880–1900.

Gideon, Crisbaum & Co., Poughkeepsie, N.Y., 1853–54.

Glass Brothers, London, Ont., c. 1880–87. London Crockery Manufacturing Co., 1887–98.
Mark, name and address impressed.

*Glassir & Co., Washington, Mo., c. 1872.

Goodale, Daniel, Jr., Hartford, Ct., at Benton & Stewart pottery, 1818–22. Goodale & Stedman, 1822–25. Goodale, solely, 1825–30.
Marks, name and address impressed.

Goodwin, Horace & Webster, Mack C., Hartford, Ct., c. 1810–40.
Mark, name and address impressed.

Goold, Franklin P., Brantford, Ont., 1859–67.
Mark, name and address impressed.

*Gossett, Amariah, Hillsboro, O., c. 1810–40.

Gray, William & Betts, Spence H., Tilsonburg, Ont., c. 1880–86. Gray & Glass, 1886–88.
Mark, name and address impressed.

*Greble, Benjamin, Baltimore, Md., 1837–50.

Green, Adam, New Brunswick, N.J., 1840–80.
Mark, name and address impressed.

*Greenland, N. W., Cassville, Pa., c. 1885–1900.

*Hall, Amos, and Cochran, Robert, Orrville, O., 1862–77.

*Hallam, David, Red Wing, Minn., 1870–72.

*Hamilton Bros., West Bridgewater, Pa., c. 1840.

*Hamilton, Clem, Tuscarawas Co., O., exact location unknown, c. 1870.
Mark, name impressed.

*Hamilton, James, Eagle Pottery, Greensboro, Pa., 1844–c. 90.
Mark, name and address, or "Eagle Pottery," usually stenciled in blue.

*Hamilton & Jones, Greensboro, Pa., c. 1870.
Mark, name and address impressed or stenciled in blue.

Hamilton, W. L., Bridgewater, Pa., c. 1837.

Hamlyn, George, Bridgeton, N.J., c. 1835–70.
George Hamlyn (II), c. 1870–1900.

Hancock, John & William, "Congress Pottery," South Amboy, N.J., 1828–c. 54.

Hanford, Isaac, Hartford, Ct., c. 1795–1805.

Hanlen, Bernard, Trenton, N.J., c. 1775–80.

Harmon, Christian, Salem, O., c. 1825–40.

Harrington, Thompson, Hartford, Ct., c. 1840–52.
Lyons, New York, 1852–72.
Marks, name and addresses impressed.

Harris, Thomas, Cuyahoga Falls, O., 1863–1900.
Mark, name impressed.

Harris, W. P., Newtown Township, O., c. 1828–56.
E. Hall, potter.
Mark, "E. Hall" and address impressed.

Hart, Charles, Sherburne, N.Y., 1841–50.
Ogdensburg, N.Y., 1850–58.
Sherburne, N.Y., 1858–c. 85.

Hart, James & Samuel, Oswego, N.Y., 1830–32.
Oswego Falls, N.Y., 1832–41.

Hart, James, Sherburne, N.Y., 1841–58.

Hart, Samuel, Oswego & Oswego Falls, N.Y., 1830–c. 65.
Also Picton, Ont., 1849–74.

Hart, William, Picton, Ont., 1849–55.
Mark, "William Hart & Co."

Hart Brothers & Lazier, Picton, Ont., 1879–c. 1905.
Mark, name (or H. B. & L.) and address.
Also, Belleville (Ont.) Stoneware Works, 1869–1904.
Marks, varied names and address.

Hastings & Belding, Ashfield, Mass., 1850–56.
Mark, name and address impressed.

Hathaway, Charles E., Somerset, Mass., 1882–c. 1900.

*Havens, Samuel, Putnam, O., c. 1836–46.

Haxstun & Co., Fort Edward, N.Y., c. 1870–c. 1900.
Later Haxstun, Ottman & Co.
Mark, name(s) and address.

*Heighshoe, S. E. Somerset, O., c. 1850.
Occasional mark, name impressed.

Henry, Jacob, Albany, N.Y., 1827–34.
Partner, C. Dillon & Co., 1834–40.

*Hewett, Isaac, Excelsior Works, Price's Landing, Pa., c. 1870–80.
Mark, name and address stenciled in blue.

*Higgins, A. D., Cleveland, O., c. 1837–50.
Occasional mark, name and address impressed.

*Hill, Foster & Co., Akron, O., c. 1849–51.
Hill, Merrill & Co., 1851–55.

*Hill, Powers & Co., Akron, O., 1859–68.
Hill & Adams, 1868–?

*Holden, Jesse, Steubenville, O., c. 1830.

*Hopkins, John, Seneca Co., O., exact location unknown, c. 1834–40.
Mark, name impressed.

*Curtis Houghton & Co., Dalton, O., 1842–64.
Houghton, Edwin, 1864–90.
Occasional mark, "Dalton Pottery" impressed.
Houghton, Eugene, 1890–1900.

Hubbell & Chesebro, Geddes (Syracuse), N.Y., 1866–83.
Mark, name and address impressed.

*Huggins & Co., Lakenan, Mo., c. 1870–80.

*Hughes, Thomas, Salem, O., 1812–c. 25.

Humiston, Perth Amboy, N.J., c. 1830–50.
Mark, name, with various partners, impressed.

*Hyssong, C. B., Cassville, Pa., c. 1870–1900.

*Iliff, Richard, Hillsboro, O., 1806–c. 20.

*Iliff, Richard, Eagle Springs (near Hillsboro), O., c. 1806.

Ingell, Jonathan W., Taunton, Mass., c. 1830–50.

*Jenkins, A., Columbus, O., c. 1840–50.

Johnson, John, Staten Island, New York, c. 1793.

*Johnson, Whitmore & Co., Akron, O., 1857–60.
Johnson & Dewey, 1860–c. 75.
Johnson & Baldwin, 1860–c. 65.

*Jones, Evan B., Pittston, Pa., c. 1880.
Mark, name and address impressed.

Judd, Norman L., Rome, N.Y., 1800–1820.

Kendall, Loammi, Chelsea, Mass., 1836–c. 70.
  Mark, name or "Chelsea" impressed.
*Kendall, Uriah, Cincinnati, O., 1834–46.
  Kendall & Sons, 1846–50.
*Kier, S.M., Pittsburgh, Pa., 1867–1900.
*Kirkpatrick, . . . , Lowell, Ill., c. 1866–1900.
*Knapp, F. K., Akron, O., 1863–85.
*Knotts, Sunderland & Co., Palatine, W. Va., c.
  1870–1900.
*Koch, . . . , Mound City, Ill., c. 1866.
*Krumeich, B. J., Newark, N.J., c. 1845–60.
  Mark, name and address impressed.

*Lambright & Westhope, New Philadelphia, O.,
  c. 1885–95.
Lathrop, Charles, Norwich, Ct., c. 1792–96.
Lazier, George, Picton, Ont., 1867–79.
  Mark, name and address impressed.
Lehman, Louis, Poughkeepsie, N.Y., 1852–56.
  Lehman & Rudinger, c. 1856–c. 58.
  Louis Lehman & Co., New York City, 1858–61.
  Marks, name and address impressed.
Lent, B., Caldwell, N.J., c. 1827.
  Mark, name and address impressed.
*Lessel, Peter, Cincinnati, O., 1848–52.
  Peter Lessel & Bro., 1852–79.
  George Lessel, 1879–99.
Letts, Joshua, Cheesequake, N.J., before 1805,
  see Warne & Letts.
Lewis & Cady, Fairfax, Vt., c. 1860.
  Mark, name and address impressed.
Lewis & Gardiner, Huntington (L.I.), N.Y., 1827–
  54.
  Marks, name and address impressed.
Lewis, W. A., Galesville, N.Y., c. 1860.
  Mark, name and address impressed.
*Link, Christian, Stonetown, Pa., c. 1870–1900.
  Mark, "Christian Link, Stonetown" impressed.
*Linton, William, Baltimore, Md., 1842–50.
Lyman, Alanson & Clark, Decius, W., Gardiner,
  Me., 1837–41.
  Mark, name and address impressed.

MacKenzie, . . . , South Woodstock, Vt., 19th
  century.

*Macomb Pottery Co., Macomb, Ill., c. 1880–1900.
Macquoid, William A., New York City, 1863–70.
  Mark, name and full address.
Macumber & Van Arsdale, Ithaca, N.Y., c. 1864.
Madden, J. M., Rondout, N.Y., c. 1870.
  Mark, name and address impressed.
Mantell, James & Thomas, Pen Yan, N.Y., c. 1850.
  Mark, name and address impressed.
*Markel, Immon & Co., Akron, O., c. 1869.
  Occasional mark, name and address impressed.
  Viall & Markell, 1869–90.
Marx, John & Hoehn, Lynden, Ont., c. 1880–95.
Mason & Russell, Cortland, N.Y., 1835–37.
  Mark, name and address impressed.
*Mayers, W. S., Roseville, O., c. 1870–80.
  Mark, name and address stenciled in blue.
*McChesney, Andrew, New Philadelphia, O., 1840–
  50.
*McConnell, . . . , Mercersburg, Pa., c. 1870–80.
*McKenzie Bros., Vanport, Pa., c. 1840–70.
*McLuney, Wm., Charleston, W. Va., c. 1809–15.
Mead, Abraham, Greenwich, Ct., c. 1785–c. 95.
*I. M. Mead & Co., Atwater, O., c. 1840–60.
  Mark, name and address.
*Meade, S., Medina Co., O., exact location un-
  known, c. 1860.
*Melleck, H. H., Roseville, O., c. 1875.
  Mark, name and address impressed.
*Merrill, Earl & Ford, Mogadore, O., c. 1880–1900.
*Merrill, Edwin H., Springfield (now part of Akron),
  O., 1835–47.
  Occasional mark, name and address impressed.
*Merrill, Edwin and Calvin, Akron, O., 1847–61.
  Edwin and Henry E. Merrill, Akron Pottery
  Co., 1861–88.
  E. H. Merrill & Co., 1888–94.
*Merrill, Powers & Co., Akron, O., 1855–58.
*Metzner, Adolph, Hamilton, O., 1884–1900.
*Miller, J., Wheeling, W. Va., c. 1869–80.
  Mark, name and address impressed.
*Miner, William, Symnes Creek, O., 1869–83.
  Mark, "Miner" impressed.
*Monmouth Pottery Co., Monmouth, Ill., 1890–
  1900.
*Monroe, J. S. and E. D., Mogadore, O., 1845–80.
Mooney, D. & Michael, Ithaca, N.Y., c. 1864.
*Moore, Alvin S., Tallmadge, O., 1850–70.

*Mootz, . . . , Putnam, O., c. 1825–40.
Morgan, David, New York City, 1794–1804.
  Mark, name and address impressed.
Morgan, James, Cheesequake, N.J., c. 1775–84.
  James Morgan, Jr., 1784–1805.
  James Morgan & Co. (Morgan, Jr. & Jacob Van Winkle), 1805–c. 30.
Morton, Justus, Brantford, Ont., 1849–56.
  Morton & Bennett, 1856–57.
  James Woodyatt & Co., 1857–58.
  Morton & Goold, 1858–59.
  Marks, names and address impressed.
Morton & Sheldon, Jordan, N.Y., c. 1860.
  Mark, "JORDAN."
*Myers, Baird & Hall, Mogadore, O., c. 1874–80.
*Myers, E. W., Mogadore, O., c. 1870.
*Myers and Hall, Mogadore, O., c. 1872.
  Occasional mark, name and address impressed.

Nash, H. & G., Utica, N.Y., 1819–28.
  Mark, name and address.
*Navarre Stoneware Co., Navarre, O., c. 1880–1900.
New York Stoneware Co., Fort Edward, N.Y., 1861–91.
  Mark, name or name and address impressed.
Nichols & Alford, Burlington, Vt., 1854–56.
  Nichols & Boynton, 1856–c. 59.
  O. L. & A. K. Ballard, c. 1859–72.
  Marks, names and address impressed.
*Nicomb, . . . , Saline Co., Ill., exact location unknown. c. 1880.
Norton, Frank B. & Hancock, Frederick, Worcester, Mass., 1858–c. 80.
  Mark after 1865, "F. B. Norton & Co./Worcester," *impressed.*
Norton, Julius, Bennington, Vt., c. 1839–43.
  Norton & Fenton, Christopher Webber, 1843–47.
  J. & E. (Edward) Norton, 1850–61.
  Edward & Luman P. Norton, c. 1858–81.
  Edward & Edward L. Norton, 1881–94.

O'Connell, R., Albany, N.Y., c. 1850.
  Marking, name and address.
*Ohio Stoneware Co., Akron, O., c. 1887.
Onondaga Pottery Co., Geddes (Syracuse), N.Y., 1871–84.

Orcutt, Eleazer, Albany, N.Y., 1842–c. 50, Troy, N.Y., 1850–60.
Orcutt, Stephen, Whately, Mass., 1797–c. 1810, with Luke & Obediah Wait, stoneware after c. 1805.
  Marks, names and address impressed.
Orcutt, Walter, Ashfield, Mass., 1848.
  Mark, "Orcutt, Guilford & Co."
  Orcutt, Belding & Co., 1849.
  Walter Orcutt & Co., 1850.
  Hastings & Belding, 1850–56.
  Marks, names and address impressed.
Orcutt, Humiston & Co., Troy, N.Y., c. 1850–60.
Orcutt & Thompson, Poughkeepsie, N.Y., c. 1860–70 (possibly not makers).

*Packer, T. A., New Philadelphia, O., c. 1875–85.
Parker, Grace (Thomas Symmes & Co.), Cambridge, Mass., 1742–46 or (52?).
*Parr, David, Baltimore, Md., 1819–34.
  David & Margaret Parr, 1834–42.
*Parr, James L. (Maryland Pottery), Baltimore, Md., 1842–50.
*Peoria Pottery Co., Peoria, Ill., 1873–94.
  Mark, on stoneware "Peoria, Illinois" *impressed, on whiteware monogram of* "P.P. Co." *printed.*
*Perrine, Maulden, Baltimore, Md., 1824–c. 50, M. Perrine & Co., c. 1850–c. 1900.
Perry, Sanford S., West Troy, N.Y., 1831–c. 65.
*Pettie, Henry & Co., Pittsburgh, Pa., c. 1860.
Pewtress, John B., Perth Amboy, N.J., c. 1840.
  Mark, name and address impressed.
*Pfaltzgraff Pottery, York, Pa., c. 1840–1900.
  Mark, "Pfaltzgraff Pottery" *impressed.*
*Philles, . . . , Red Wing, Minn., 1872–77.
*Phillips, Moro, Wilsons Landing, Va., Philadelphia, Pa., 1853–67.
  Camden, N.J., 1867–97.
Phoris, C., Co., Geddes (Syracuse), N.Y., c. 1861–66.
  Mark, name and address impressed.
Pierson & Horn; Wood, William; Swift, Charles, Gardiner, Me., 1875–c. 1900.
Pitkin, Richard & Woodbridge, Dudley, Manchester, Ct., 1800–c. 1820.
Pierson, Andrew, Bangor Stoneware Works, Bangor, Me., c. 1890–1916.

Plaisted, F. A., Gardiner, Me., 1850–74.
Mark, name and address impressed.
*Pohl, Joseph, Red Wing, Minn., c. 1858–70.
Pottman Bros., Fort Edward, N.Y., c. 1870.
Mark, name and address impressed.
Potts, Christopher & Son, Norwich, Ct., 1796–97. Later proprietors unknown; pottery closed in 1816.
Price, Abial, Middletown Point, N.J., 1847–52.
Mark, name and address impressed.
Price, Xerxes, Sayreville (Roundabout), N.J., c. 1802.
Mark, name, address and "Roundabout" impressed, or initials "X. P." incised.
Pruden, John, Elizabeth, New Jersey, 1816–79.
Mark, name and address impressed.
Pruden, John M., Jr., Elizabeth, N.J., 1835–79.
Mark, name and address impressed.
*Purdy, Solomon, Atwater, O., c. 1850.
Mark, "S. Purdy," with or without "Portage Co." or "Atwater," impressed.
Purdy, Gordon B., 1860–70.
Occasional mark, name impressed.
Purdy, Fitzhugh; Purdy & Loomis.
Mark, name impressed.

*Quigley, S., Cincinnati, O., c. 1834.
Mark, "S. Quigley, Franklin Factory, Cincinnati, O." impressed.
Quinn, E. H., Brooklyn, N.Y., c. 1860.

*Read, Thomas, New Philadelphia, O., c. 1850–65.
Mark, "T. Read" impressed.
*Red Wing Stoneware Co., Red Wing, Minn., 1872–1900.
Reidinger & Caire, Adam, Poughkeepsie, N.Y., 1856–96.
Mark, name impressed.
*Reiss, William, Wilmington, Del., c. 1851.
Remmey, Henry (I), Philadelphia, Pa., 1810–35.
Remmey, Henry H. (II), Baltimore, Md., c. 1818–35.
Philadelphia, Pa., c. 1835–59.
Remmey (Henry H. II) & Burnet, Philadelphia, Pa., c. 1840.
Remmey, Joseph Henry, South Amboy, N.J., c. 1818–23.

Remmey, John (III), New York City, 1799–1814.
Mark, "J. Remmey/Manhattan Wells/New York."
*Remmey, Richard C., Philadelphia, Pa., 1859–1900.
Mark, initials or name impressed.
*Reynolds, . . . , Owensboro, Ind., c. 1869.
*Rice, Prosper, Putnam, O., 1827–50.
Mark on stoneware, name impressed.
*Rich, . . . , Roscoe, O., c. 1870.
Mark, name impressed.
*Richey & Hamilton, Palatine, W. Va., c. 1875.
Mark, name and address stenciled in blue.
*Riggs, Wesley, Sandyville, O., c. 1820–30.
Risley, Sidney, Norwich, Ct., c. 1846–75.
George L., 1875–81.
Norwich Pottery Works, 1881–95.
Marks, names and address impressed.
*Robbins, Mrs. and Son, Calhoun, Mo., c. 1873.
Roberts, William Binghamton, N.Y., c. 1857–82.
Mark, name and address impressed.
*Rockwell, W. H. & Co., Akron, O., 1860–90.
Rowley Pottery, Akron, O., c. 1874.
*Royer, A. Akron, O., c. 1865–75.
Russell, Andrew J., Troy, N.Y., c. 1870–78.

Sables, T. & Co. (Thomas and John), Medford, Mass., 1838–44.
Sage, J. & Co., Cortland, N.Y., c. 1870.
Mark, name and address impressed.
*St. Louis Stoneware Co., St. Louis, Mo., 1865–1900.
Sandford, Peter Peregrine, Hackensack, N.J., c. 1789.
Mark, name incised.
Satterlee & Mory, Fort Edward, N. Y., 1861–91, as New York Stoneware Co.
Marks, both names and address.
*Schenefelder, Daniel P., Reading, Pa., 1869–1900.
Mark, name and address impressed.
*Schenkle, William, Excelsior Pottery, Akron, O., 1870–75.
Schenkle Bros. & Mann, 1875–c. 85.
*Schofield & Co., D. G., New Brighton, Pa., c. 1877–93.
Schrieber, John, Rondout, N.Y., c. 1870.
Mark, name and "Rondout."
Schuler & McGlade, Paris, Ont., c. 1866–c. 80.
*Scott, George, Cincinnati, O., 1846–89.
George Scott & Sons, 1889–1900.

Seaver, William, Taunton, Mass., c. 1790–1815.
John & William, Jr., 1815–c. 30.
Selby, Edward, Albany, N.Y., partner in C. Dillon & Co., 1834–c. 36.
Hudson, N.Y., c. 1836–?
Selby, Edward & Son, West Troy, N.Y., c. 1876.
Seymour, George R., West Troy, N.Y., c. 1845–60.
Seymour, Israel, Troy, N.Y., 1819–65.
Mark, name and address impressed.
Seymour, Orson H., Hartford, Ct.; *see*, Webster, Mack C.
Seymour & Brother, 1867–71.
Seymour & Bosworth, 1873–c. 90.
Marks, names and address impressed.
Seymour, Walter J., Troy, N.Y., 1852–c. 85.
*Seymour & Stedman, Ravenna, O., c. 1850.
Mark, name and address impressed.
*Sheldon, F. L., Mogadore, O., 1845–78.
Shepard, Joseph, Jr., Geddes (Syracuse), N.Y., 1858–c. 61.
Shepley & Smith, West Troy, N.Y., c. 1865–95.
*Shorb, Adam L., Canton, O., 1840–c. 60.
*Shorb, J., Jr., Canton, O., 1817–24.
Shorb, Adam A., 1824–c. 50.
*Simns, N. M., East Liverpool, O., 1869–70.
Skinner, Samuel, Picton, Ont., 1855–67.
Mark, "S. Skinner & Co."
Smith, Asa E., Norwalk, Ct., 1825–37.
Selleck & Smith, 1837–43.
Smith & Day, 1843–c. 50.
A. E. Smith & Sons, c. 1850–87.
Marks, names and address impressed.
*Smith, A., Springfield (now part of Akron), O., c. 1870.
*Smith, H. S., Gamesville, Mo., c. 1890.
*Smith, J. C., Mogadore, O., c. 1862.
Mark, name and address impressed.
Smith, Washington, Greenwich (L.I.), N.Y., 1834–50.
*Smith, Willoughby, Wrightstown (near Womelsdorf), Pa., 1862–1900.
Mark, "W. Smith," "Smith," or "Womelsdorf" impressed.
*Smyth, Joel, Smyth & Harmell, Paris, O., c. 1840.
*Snyder, Henry, Millersburg, O., c. 1875–85.
Somerset Pottery, Pottersville & Boston, Mass., 1882–1909.

Marks "L. & B. C. Chace/Somerset" or "Somerset Potters Works."
*Somerset Pottery Works, Somerset, N.J., c. 1875.
Mark, name impressed.
*Sowers, H., Roseville, O., c. 1887.
*Spafford & Richards, Akron, O., 1870–95.
Standish, Alexander, Taunton, Mass., 1846–c. 70.
Mark, name (Standish & Wright to 1855), and address impressed.
Starkey & Howard, Keene, N.H., 1871–75.
States, Adam, Greenwich, Ct., 1749–c. 67.
States, Adam (& Sons), Stonington, Ct., c. 1767–1835.
States, Peter, Stonington, Ct., c. 1767–?
States, William, Long Point, Ct., 1811–23.
Stedman, Absalom, & Seymour, Frederick(?), Hartford, Ct., 1825–c. 35.
Mark, name and address impressed.
*Stevens, Joseph P., Harris, James; Danas, John; Martin's Ferry, O., c. 1840.
*S. L. Stoll & Co., Mogadore, O., 1864–c. 80.
*Stoneware and Tile Co., Louisville, O., 1880–1900.
*Straw, Michael, Greensburg, Pa., c. 1837.
Swan & States (Joshua Swan & Ichabod States), Long Point (Stonington), Ct., 1823–35.
Mark, name and address impressed.
*Swank, Hiram & Sons, Johnstown, Pa., c. 1865–1900.
Mark, name and address, impressed or stenciled in blue.
Synan, Patrick & William, Somerset, Mass., 1893–1912.

Taft, James Scholly, Keene, N.H., 1871–c. 80.
*Thomas, J. R., Cuyahoga Falls, O., 1857–87.
Thomas Bros., 1887–1900.
Titus, Jonathon, Huntington (L.I.), N.Y., c. 1785–1805.
*Tourpet & Becker, Brazil, Ind., 1859–1900.
Tracy, Andrew & Huntington, Norwich, Ct., 1786–98.
Hosmer, Joseph, 1798–1800.
Cleveland, William, 1800–1814.
Armstrong & Wentworth, 1814–34.
*Tracy, Nelson, New Philadelphia, O., c. 1865–75.
Tracy, John B., c. 1875–90.

*Tupper, C., Portage Co., O., exact location unknown, c. 1870.
Mark, name impressed.
*Turley Bros., Burlington, Ia., 1870–1900.
Tyler, Moses, Albany, N.Y., 1826–48.
Mark, "TYLER & DILLON" to 1834; "M. TYLER, ALBANY/MANUFACTURER" to 1848.
*Tyron, Wright & Co., Tallmadge, O., 1868–75.

Underwood, J. A. & C. W., Fort Edward, N.Y., c. 1870–80.
Mark, name and address impressed.
Union Pottery (Haidle & Co.), Haidle, Conrad & Sonn, John C., Newark, N.J., 1871–75.
Haidle & Zipf, 1875–77.
*United States Stoneware Co., Akron, O., 1885–1900.

Van Schoik, Joseph & Dunn, Ezra, Middletown Point, N.J., 1852–59.
Dunn, Dunlop & Co., 1859–?
Mark, name and address impressed.
Van Winckle, Jacob, Cheesequake, N.J., c. 1800–c. 1830, *see* James Morgan.
Van Winckle, Nicholas, Herbertsville, N.J., 1823–c. 40.
*Vandemark, John, Frazeesburg Road, O., c. 1840–50.
Vaupel, Cornelius, Brooklyn, N.Y., 1877–86.
Mark, name and address impressed.

*Wagoner Bros., Vanport, Pa., c. 1860–70.
Mark, name and address impressed.
Wait, Luke & Obediah, Whately, Mass., c. 1810–30.
*Wait & Ricketts, Springfield (now part of Akron), O., c. 1870.
Occasional mark, name and address impressed.
Wands, I. W., Olean, N.Y., 1852–c. 70.
Mark, name impressed.
Warne, Thomas, Cheesequake (South Amboy), N.J., c. 1800–1805.
Mark, name and address impressed.
Warne, Thomas & Letts, Joshua, Cheesequake, N.J., c. 1805–13.
Mark varied, initials or name and address impressed.

Warner, William E., Columbian Pottery, Perth Amboy, N.J., c. 1830–35.
West Troy, N.Y., c. 1835–c. 70.
Marks, name and address impressed.
Warner, W. E. & Co., Toronto, Ont., c. 1856–70.
Mark, name and address impressed.
*Washington Stoneware Co., Washington, Mo., c. 1897.
*Watson, J. R., Perth Amboy, N.J., c. 1833–40.
*Weaver, James L., Roseville, O., c. 1877.
*Webster, Elijah, East Liverpool, O., 1859–64.
Webster, Mack C., with Horace Goodwin, Hartford, Ct., c. 1810–40.
M. C. Webster & Son, 1840–57.
Charles T. Webster & Orson Seymour, 1857–c. 67.
Marks, names and address impressed.
*Weeks, Cook & Weeks, Akron, O., 1882–1900.
Occasional mark, name and address in relief on bottom.
*Weise, Henry, Hagerstown, Md., c. 1870, earlier Martinsburg, W. Va.
Welding & Belding, Brantford, Ont., 1867–72.
Welding, W. E., 1873–94.
Marks, names and address impressed.
*Welker, Adam, Massillon, O., c. 1860–85.
*Weller, Samuel, Fultonham, O., 1873–1900.
Wells, Ashbel, Hartford, Ct., c. 1785–c. 1800.
Wells, Crafts & Wells, Whately, Mass., 1849–51.
Mark, name and address impressed.
*Wells, Joseph, Wellsville, O., 1826–c. 35.
*Wells, S., Wellsville, O., c. 1835–56.
West Troy Pottery, West Troy, N.Y., c. 1870–80.
Mark, name impressed.
*West Virginia Pottery Co., Bridgeport, W. Va., 1880–1900.
*Western Stoneware Co., Monmouth, Ill., 1870–90.
White & Wood, Binghamton, N.Y., 1883–87.
Mark, name and address impressed.
White, Noah, Utica, N.Y., 1828–40.
Noah White & Sons, 1840–53.
N. White & Co., Binghamton, N.Y., 1859–83.
Noah White, Jr., Utica & Binghamton to c. 1885.
Varied marks, name and address impressed.
*Whiteman, T. W., Perth Amboy, N.J., c. 1860–70.
Whitman, J. M., Havana, N.Y., c. 1860–70.
Mark, name and address impressed.

*Whitman, Robinson & Co., Akron, O., c. 1862–86.

Whittemore, R. O., Havana, N.Y., c. 1860–c. 80.
Mark, name and address impressed.

Willard & Sons, Ballardville, Mass., c. 1880–95.
Mark, name and address impressed or "Ballardville Stoneware Manufacturing Co."

*Williams & McCoy, Roseville, O., 1886–1900.

*Winfel, R., Perry, Mo., c. 1876.

Wingender, Charles, Sr. & Jr., Haddonfield, N.J., 1890–1904.
Mark, address over name, impressed.

Winslow, John T., Portland, Me., 1846–?
Mark, name and address impressed.

Woodruff, Madison, Cortland, N.Y., 1849–c. 90.
Mark, name or name and address impressed.

Woolworth, F., Burlington, Vt. (Ballard Pottery), 1872–95. Later proprietor H. E. Sulls.
Marks, names and address impressed.

*Wores, H., Dover, O., c. 1825–46.
Mark, name impressed.

*Works, Laban H., New Philadelphia, O., c. 1845.
Mark, "L. H. Works" impressed.

Worthen, C. F., Peabody, Mass., c. 1870.
Mark, name and address impressed.

Wright, Alexander, Tauton, Mass. with Alexander Standish, 1846–55, Barnstable Mass., c. 1860.

*Young, Samuel, Martin's Ferry, O., c. 1850.

Zipf, Jacob, Union Pottery, Newark, N.J., 1877–c. 1906.

Glossary

BARTMANNKRUG: the German term for brown salt-glazed jugs of the 16th and 17th centuries, decorated with bearded masks in relief. The English term for the same jugs was "bellarmine."

BLUE GLAZED: decorative glazing in cobalt-blue.

BRUSH GLAZED: colored glaze as a liquid applied to pottery by brush.

BUSHING: the socket or fitting applied as a separate piece, to strengthen the spigot opening in a water cooler, and provide a socket for a wooden spigot.

CAPACITY FIGURE or MARKING: the number, either stamped or painted in blue glaze, on many vessels to indicate capacity in gallons.

COCKSPUR: a small piece of clay, often roughly formed, used as a separator between pieces of pottery being fired.

COGGLE: a small wheel bearing an intaglio design, used for transferring that design as a relief band to newly formed soft pottery.

COOLER: a large jug or cask, usually with a spigot, for serving water, cider, or beer from a bar or counter.

DOUBLE FIRING: the process of firing biscuit (unglazed) pottery, then glazing and/or decorating and refiring.

DRY GLAZE: glaze mixed and applied to pottery as a dry powder rather than a liquid.

FOUNTAIN: almost synonymous with cooler.

GLAZE: any hard ceramic coating based on a mixture of silica and a metallic oxide or salt. Glazes are not ceramic, but rather are forms of glass.

GREENWARE: formed pottery which is air dried but unfired and thus still raw clay.

PORRINGER: a small handled bowl or large shallow cup, an all-purpose eating vessel before the 19th century.

PUG-MILL: a device somewhat like a modern blender, but much larger and usually horse driven, for refining and mixing clay.

PULLED-HANDLE: a handle of clay drawn from the body of a vessel, rather than a piece separately applied.

QUILL TRAILING: trailing slip or glaze from a slip-cup and through a quill, for decorative banding or figures.

RIB: a wooden scraper or forming die, used for smoothing sides and forming rims of pots.

ROPE OF CLAY: two or three cylindrical pieces of clay twisted together to form a clay rope, usually as a decorative handle.

SAGGER: usually an enclosed container, but with North American stoneware, a roughly formed base for pottery during firing.

SANDER: a desk sander, for sprinkling sand on wet ink before paper blotters.

SGRAFFITO DECORATED: a decoration by incising into raw pottery through an unfired glaze.

227

SLIP: a ceramic coating of refined clay rather than glaze. The term "slip" can also apply to clay sufficiently liquid for casting in molds rather than turning on a wheel.

SLIP-CUP: a cup with straw or quill nozzle, for applying lines of slip or glaze.

SMOOTHER: either a wooden paddle for smoothing the sides of wet, freshly turned pottery, or the person whose job it was to smooth out turning marks on pottery with a wet cloth.

SWAG: a decorative motif with the appearance of draped or swagged fabric.

THROWER: the primary pottery fabricator; the man who turned pots on a wheel.

WEDGE: a separator used for lateral separation of pots in firing. Stoneware wedges are shaped somewhat like flat-ended bones, and as a form seem unique to North American stoneware production.

Bibliography

ANDRADE, CYRIL: "The Early Pottery of England," *The Antiquarian*, October 1929, pp. 58–59 ff.

BARBEAU, MARIUS: "Canadian Pottery," *Antiques*, June 1941, pp. 296–99

BARBER, EDWIN ATLEE: *Pottery and Porcelain in the United States*, Putnam, New York, 1893

———: *The Tulip ware of the Pennsylvania German Potters*, Pennsylvania Museum, Philadelphia, 1903

———: *Marks of American Potters*, Patterson & White, Philadelphia, 1904

———: *Salt Glazed Stoneware*, Pennsylvania Museum, Philadelphia, 1906

BARRET, RICHARD CARTER: *Bennington Pottery and Porcelain: A Guide to Identification*, Bonanza, New York, 1958

BLACKER, J. F.: *The A B C of English Salt-Glaze Stoneware*, Stanley Paul, London, 1922

BLAIR, C. DEAN: *The Potters and Potteries of Summit County Ohio, 1828–1915*, Summit County Historical Society, Akron, 1965

BRITISH MUSEUM: *A Guide to the English Pottery and Porcelain in the Department of Ceramics and Ethnography*, London, 1923

BURLINGTON FINE ARTS CLUB (Glaisher, J. W. L.) Catalog: *Exhibition of Early English Earthenware*, Burlington Fine Arts Club, London, 1914

CLARK, NATHAN: Miscellaneous manuscripts and accounts, New York State Historical Association, Cooperstown, N.Y.

CLEMENT, ARTHUR W.: *Notes on American Ceramics, 1607–1943*, Brooklyn Museum & Brooklyn Institute of Arts and Sciences, 1944

———: *Our Pioneer Potters*, privately published, New York, 1947

COLLARD, ELIZABETH A.: *Nineteenth-Century Pottery and Porcelain in Canada*, McGill, Montreal, 1967

Documents Relative to the Manufactures in the United States, 2 vols., Washington, D.C., 1833

"The Glass and China Cupboard—American Ceramics," *Antiques*, February 1944, pp. 86–89

HAYDEN, ARTHUR: *Chats on English Earthenware*, Unwin, London, 1909

HOBSON, R. L.: *Catalog of English Pottery* (in the British Museum), British Museum, London, 1903

HODGES, HENRY: *Artifacts: An Introduction to Early Materials and Technology*, John Baker, London, 1964

HODGKIN, J. E. and E.: *Examples of Early English Earthenwares, Named, Dated, and Described*, Cassel, London, 1891

HOUGH, WALTER: "An Early West Virginia Pottery," *Annual Report of the U.S. National Museum* (for 1899), Washington, D.C., 1901

HUME, IVOR NOËL: "German Stoneware Bellarmines —An Introduction," *Antiques*, November 1958, pp. 439–41

———: "Rhenish Gray Stonewares in Colonial America," *Antiques*, September 1967, pp. 349–53

———: *Here Lies Virginia*, Knopf, New York, 1963

MONMOUTH COUNTY HISTORICAL ASSOCIATION: *New Jersey Stoneware*, Catalog of an exhibition (on May 21–June 21, 1955)

NELSON, BORIS E.: *The Potter's Art, c. 1680–c. 1900*. Catalog of an exhibition at the New Jersey State

Museum, (Jan. 24–Sept. 3, 1956), Trenton, 1956

NEWARK MUSEUM ASSOCIATION: *The Work of the Potteries of New Jersey from 1685 to 1876,* Newark, N.J., 1914

PITKIN, ALBERT H.: *Early American Folk Pottery,* Case, Lockwood & Brainard, Hartford, Connecticut., 1918

PRIME, ALFRED C.: *Arts and Crafts in Philadelphia, Maryland, and North Carolina,* New York Historical Society, New York, 1938

RACKHAM, BERNARD, and READ, HERBERT: *English Pottery,* Benn, London, 1924

RAMSAY, JOHN: *American Potters and Pottery,* Hale, Cushman & Flint, Boston, 1939

RAYMOND, W. OAKLEY: "Colonial and Early American Earthenware," *The Antiquarian,* January 1928

———: "Unmarked New York Pottery: Crolius and Remmey," *The Antiquarian,* January 1930, pp. 54–55 ff.

REMENSNYDER, JOHN P.: "The Potters of Poughkeepsie," *Antiques,* July 1966, pp. 90–95

RICE, A. H. and STROUDT, J. B.: *The Shenandoah Pottery,* Shenandoah Publishing Co., Strasburg, Va., 1929

RIES, HEINRICH: *History of the Clay-Working Industry in the United States,* Wiley, New York, 1909

SAMMIS, MRS. IRVING: "The Pottery at Huntington, Long Island," *Antiques,* April 1923, pp. 161–65

SCOON, CAROLYN: "New York State Stoneware in the New York Historical Society," New York Historical Society *Quarterly Bulletin,* April 1945, pp. 83–91

SIM, ROBERT J., and CLEMENT, ARTHUR W.: "The Cheesequake Potteries," *Antiques,* March 1944, pp. 122–25

SOLON, M. L.: *The Ancient Art Stoneware of the Low Countries and Germany,* 2 vols., London, 1892

SPARGO, JOHN: *The Potters and Potteries of Bennington,* Houghton Mifflin, Boston, 1926

———: *Early American Pottery and China,* Century Co., New York, 1926

———: "The Fentons: Pioneer American Potters," *Antiques,* October 1923, pp. 166–69

STOW, CHARLES MESSNER: "The 'Deacon Potter' of Greenwich," *The Antiquarian,* March 1930, pp. 46–47 ff.

TAYLOR, DAVID and PATRICIA: *The Hart Pottery, Canada West,* Picton Gazette Publishing Co., Picton, Ont., 1966

WATKINS, C. M. and HUME, I. N.: *The Poor Potter of Yorktown,* Bulletin 249, U.S. National Museum, Washington, 1967

WATKINS, LAURA WOODSIDE: *Early New England Potters and Their Wares,* Harvard Univ. Press, Boston, 1950

———: *Early New England Pottery,* Old Sturbridge Village, 1959

———: "The Stoneware of South Ashfield, Massachusetts," *Antiques,* September 1934 pp. 94–97

WEBSTER, DONALD BLAKE: *The Brantford Pottery, 1849–1907,* Royal Ontario Museum, Toronto, 1968

WHEELER, ROBERT C.: "A Checklist of Albany Potters," *New York History,* October 1944

———: "The Potters of Albany," *Antiques,* December 1944, pp. 345–47

WILLIAMSON, SCOTT GRAHAM: *The American Craftsman,* Crown, New York, 1940

WILLIS, KATHERINE: "Founders of Early American Pottery," *The Antiquarian,* August 1928, pp. 33–35

Index

Numbers in roman refer to the text; those in italic refer to captions.